Family Theology
Finding God in Very Human Relationships

CAROL J. GALLAGHER

Morehouse Publishing

NEW YORK · HARRISBURG · DENVER

Revised Standard Version of the Bible, copyright 1952 (2nd edition, 1971) by the Division of Christian Education of the National Council of the Churches of Christ in the United States of America. Used by permission. All rights reserved.

Morehouse Publishing, 4775 Linglestown Road, Harrisburg, PA 17112

Morehouse Publishing, 445 Fifth Avenue, New York, NY 10016

Morehouse Publishing is an imprint of Church Publishing Incorporated.

www.churchpublishing.org

Cover design by Laurie Klein Westhafer
Typeset by Denise Hoff

Library of Congress Cataloging-in-Publication Data

Gallagher, Carol.
  Family theology : finding God in very human relationships /
Carol J. Gallagher.
      p. cm.
  ISBN 978-0-8192-2437-8 (pbk.) -- ISBN 978-0-8192-2455-2 (ebook)
1. Families--Religious aspects--Christianity. I. Title.
  BT707.7.G35 2012
  261.8'3585--dc23
                            2012012220

Printed in the United States of America

10 9 8 7 6 5 4 3 2 1

❧ **Contents** ❧

❧ **Dedication** ❧

This book is dedicated to my beloved husband Mark, who has helped me through every challenge bringing laughter and joy to the darkest places; my beloved daughters Emily, Ariel, and Phoebe, who are my heart and my all, and to Lillian our beautiful granddaughter, who has started love anew; to my mother, Betty WalkingStick Theobald, who has given us more than we can ever return; to my siblings, Sherry, Don, and Betsy who put up with all my shenanigans and love me still; and to all my Point friends who helped me grow in faith and love by playing guitars late into the night and staring up with wonder at the stars.

This book is also offered in memory of father, the Rev. Donald K. Theobald, who lived his faith large and loud; my sister Pegi, who taught me harmony and imagination; and to all the family saints above who have gone to their rest and are embedded in the arms of their loving Creator.

~ Introduction ~

We all are born into families. Each family of origin is embedded in a community that shares traditions that shape who we are together and speak to the bedrock issues of our life together including our notions of God. Our larger family units define the values and traditions which the entire group or village honors. In our specific communal cultural contexts we learn our gender roles as small girls and boys and these roles also inform us about our relationship with God. Though each of us gives individual witness to whom we know God to be, that knowledge is first shaped by the stories of our various communities.

The language in which we best receive God is the language of family and relationship. When people hear the word "theology" they often think of it as an academic exercise, which is not necessarily immediately considered a creative process. Theology is not often listed among the course work in academies that teach painting, creative writing, and dance. Theologians, who sometimes speak separated from a church community, tend to want to talk about God in the abstract, overlooking the ringing reality that we know God first and foremost through personal and communal experience. While they give intellectual assent to God as ultimate Creator, Primary Progenitor, Parent-par-Excellence, they fail to incarnate that same creativity in their work, studying about the Creator, rather than co-creating. Theologians who choose to be great and respected academics thus become distant from their own personal contexts and creations. The messy soup of their own families is often at an intellectual polarity from God rather than an entrance into the heart of the Creator.

Preachers, teachers, and church leaders—ministers who live out their lives in community—also begin by seeing God as the Creator and Sustainer of all life who uses creation's raw materials to fashion a glorious world. Their challenge is to carry the creative energy of theological reflection and bring it to life in the daily rituals and conversations of the community, theological or otherwise. The more we hear the invitation from God to be creative and to learn from life, the better we can look at our own tapestry, our own painting, and understand the depth of God's love for us and the creative meaning we can make within the messy context from which all the abundance of life is derived.

In this book I have chosen to look at how the real lived lives of present-day folks intersect with the Bible stories we read even though we are distant in time and thought from the culture and context in which these stories were lived out. Whether we are from a repressive or very liberal society, a patriarchal or matrilineal society, or a polyglot of cultural and religious contexts, we can find ways to connect with the people we read about in the scriptures. There are truths about God and ourselves we share with them, even though they lived in very different worlds and with radically different self-understandings than we assume for ourselves. Over time and distance we are called to find the truth in the stories both from historical reality and from the lived experience of God with us today. We are invited to find ways to make connections to our own lived experience. Our God-given creative capacity is where ancient and modern collide without bumpers and where the mashed-up bits of scripture and experience coalesce into a new, more complex creation for our times, for our lives. This book is an invitation to tears and laughter, to storytelling and self-revelation. You are invited to meet God in your very own time and space, and to find God in the family stories passed down through history. We are all invited by God to know and be known as part of a unique and changing family, as beloved individuals created in the image and likeness of God in our time and this place.

The voice you will hear throughout this book will be the voice of a Native-American woman who is a wife, mother, grandmother, and Bishop in the Episcopal Church. I have several degrees in theology and have taught in several seminaries, but my focus here is less concerned with solely intellectual pursuits and instead aims to reveal the more personal, and more relational aspects of our lives. My take on these biblical stories will be offered with a good dose of playfulness and teasing. In my Cherokee tradition, when we care for something or someone, they are subject to a considerable amount of play and teasing. So, following that tradition, I will tease and play with the familiar words of scripture in order to have robust relationship with the scripture and the reader.

I also expect that some will find my interaction with scripture jarring, troubling, and sometimes annoying. I am all those things. When I engage the Scriptures, I try to bring my whole humanity into the exercise. I truly believe that God dwells with us most viscerally when we are fully human, expressing our anger and shame, our joys and sorrows, our completely magnificent and wonderfully broken humanity.

Creating God

In the chaos and in stillness I am
in the silvery light at morning's edge
I am breathing life for those lost wretched
I am singing for those who have forgotten
I am dancing for the lame and I am.

From feeble relationships to mighty nations I am
guiding and instructing patient I am
floods and hurricanes and miracle babies I am
children rushing unwilling to hold back
love I am.

For beauty and folly, for inky nights I am
bright days and twisted smiles laughing I am
creating and recreating love new mornings I am.

based on John 8:48–59

Basic Theological Assumptions

In most every Bible story we receive, God's work is not complete until one child redeems another, until one man or one woman gives their life for their people, and when one nation brings salvation for all. God's work in the historical narrative is redemptive and God's work is redemptive in our time. God's story is a story of regular and constant redemption, and of renewed relationships healed after horrible frays in the fabric of life. God's story is the meta-narrative of our story: the big, over-encompassing tale that binds us together in all sorts of relationships, all sorts of families, and all kinds of tribal communities.

As we move through the texts together we will see that the work of God is not complete until a human being participates in the creative drama. Not until Joseph redeems his brothers and their families along with their father is the story fulfilled and complete in the eyes of the Creator. More than just his immediate family, Joseph was to save his whole community, the foreign land in which he was a captive slave and the nations that bordered their world. God's work is not complete when might or right wins out, but only when redemption and reconciliation are complete. God's creativity and God's story are found within the spiraling human circle of betrayal and redemption that is born out of both nurturing and contentious familial relations. It is the story too of our relationship with God, a continuing and regular dance in which we are not bystanders but active participants. The story of the Prodigal Son, for example, is as much about the older brother and the work he has to do to know God's activity in his life, as it is about an obnoxious younger brother. "Son, everything I have is yours": the redemption and reconciliation of all God's children is everyone's work and no one can say we are not family. We cannot cast one another aside as accidents or mistakes of misguided parents.

Historical Awareness

When asked, I have often offered my insight to the debate over same sex marriage by remarking that up until very recent history marriage was a contract between two men. Wives and children have been considered commodities, counted on a list of household possessions when a man's life was inventoried. Our present American accepted view of sexual equality and value is not only not universal at present, but was never accepted in the past, including the family stories from the Bible.

Today, we are blessed in America to live in a time when few children die at birth and in infancy. Both mother and child routinely died in childbirth up until the very recent past in this country; the wonderful prenatal and postnatal care now offered routinely was unknown to previous generations. The present reality across much of our globe is that mothers and babies die all the time and maternal health care is not considered an important issue in many countries. Our ancestors had children to ensure the survival of the family business or the family farm and the essential to the existence of the household. Young children were put to work and expected to do their part. Childhood did not really exist; growing up did. Taking your place among the people and growing strong to lend a hand was at the center of the relationship between parent and child, between the community and its children.

We can only imagine, therefore, what it was like to be a child in a household in ancient Israel or Palestine. The tools of historical research help us understand better how life was lived, but much is still open to interpretation. The purpose of this book is not to reconstruct the past, but to find intersections between the stories in scripture and our present lives. The biblical accounts offer us insight as we explore our own stories, our own relationships, and our places in the midst of God's story, just as the ancient ones did. We can find the threads of common human existence, the things that make us laugh and cry, the isolations and intimacies, the expectations and harsh realities, and connect with those across history who were seeking to know God.

Over the centuries of Christian history, theologians have studied God and offered many theories about God and Jesus Christ. Liberation theologians, neo-orthodox, and everybody in between have struggled to describe God and explain our relationship to our Creator. The work we will be doing in this book joins that work engaging both Hebrew and Christian scriptures as living testaments to God's love and ongoing creative and renewing activity in the lives of human beings, those of us made of flesh and walking on this planet. In this complicated generation of global warming and ever-increasing religious conflict, this book offers a simple method by which to examine our lives and find God within our humble, challenging, and often broken relationships.

The American religious experience and much of the practice of faith in our religious institutions reflect a strident individualism. Many people believe that their life of faith is between them and their God, and the family and community are secondary at best. There are many theological voices from the across the world that challenge that understanding and can also help us move from an individual in relationship with God to a more complex vision that encompasses family, culture, and context. Liberation Theology invites us to hear the Gospel with the ears of the poor. Gustavo Gutierrez writes:

"But the poor person does not exist as an inescapable fact of destiny. His or her existence is not politically neutral, and it is not ethically innocent. The poor are a by-product of the system in which we live and for which we are responsible. They are marginalized by our social and cultural world. They are the oppressed, exploited proletariat, robbed of the fruit of their labor and despoiled of their humanity. Hence the poverty of the poor is not a call to generous relief action, but a demand that we go and build a different social order." [1]

As a nation of immigrants, many Americans can trace their origins through an historical port of entry. Their predecessors were

---

[1] *We Drink from Our Own Wells: The Spiritual Journey of People* (Maryknoll, NY: Orbis, 1984, 2003), 20.

simply identified as the "tired, the poor yearning to be free"—people who were destitute, running from death, poverty, and oppression. Those of us who trace our heritage from the indigenous people of this land, the tribal people who welcomed these immigrants to our shores, share ancestors who also suffered as a population from extreme poverty, disease, and oppression.

Robert Warrior (Osage), who is professor of American Indian Studies, and who has written extensively about the Indigenous experience in the Americas, suggests that the American Indian can be considered as the Canaanites, Native people as the despised people who God's people wiped out by right and might, taking the land that was "flowing with milk and honey." When the first European settlers arrived on the North American continent, their self-given mandate grew out of their enmeshed identification with the ancient biblical stories, seeing themselves as arriving in a new Jerusalem, some assuming that this land was chosen for them by God. Their sense of spiritual destiny caused them to oppress and dislocate others.

Family Theology is an invitation to engage the source of our faith, the scriptures, and, at the same time, to understand the many influences and relationships that affect the way we read the scripture and practice our faith. We each have unique experiences in family, community, and in our relations with the wider world. We carry these experiences into our understanding of God. Faith is never really and completely personal, but is always found in context. We are encouraged to understand family as a larger circle, an ever widening scope that helps us find our place and make authentic connections with God and one another.

Family Theology requires an honest reflection on one's self, one's family, and one's community, all of which demand a willingness to be simultaneously personal and public, humble and creative. We are invited to remember ourselves as children, to play with the images and stories we read, and to find a way to see ourselves within the stories of God. We are to weave our new stories into the ancient and constant faithfulness of God's people and God's family. There is no one who is outside the scope of stories that are the evidence of the living God. This work can be painful and confusing about the nature of God, especially for those who want clear answers from theology. The promise of this work is an authentic and living understanding of God's activity within every person, family, and community. Long before we find God in a structure, a worship space, or in Sunday School, we find God in the face of a loving parent, or perhaps in the tender touch of grandparent.

For many folks, including myself, the experience of a loving family has been compromised by many things—including mental illness, physical, mental, and sexual abuse, as well as substance abuse of all kinds. The victims of abuse within a family can find it hard to love and trust God and other human beings. God is especially caring of those who suffer abuse. The Scriptures, over and over again, point to a loving Creator who seeks justice, restoration, and healing and a Divine source that sides always with the marginalized, battered, and abused.

My Family of Origin

I am the third daughter of four and the fourth child of five; my brother hovers in the middle of all these girls who span seventeen years. My father, Donald Theobald, was a Presbyterian Minister and long-time Navy Chaplain (full Commander at retirement) and fifty-two years ordained at the time of his death. He raised us with rules and chores. He liked us to work together, to sing and play instruments together, to study scripture together, and to move as a unit, all together. He was an only child. There was very little "us" in his growing up and he set out to create the biggest tribal group he could summon.

Marrying my mother, Elizabeth WalkingStick, made him not only adopted into a tribe by marriage but also blended in with a matriarchal and matrilineal Cherokee tribe with all of the problems and identity issues that plagued Native Americans in the 20th century and continue to our present day. My mother was born in Oklahoma and was sent east as her family was being torn apart by the alcohol abuse and violence that marked those years of the Dust Bowl, the oil boom, and the subsequent oil bust. It was wild country during those years, as oil made people lust after money and devalue human life. The many tribes that had been brought to Oklahoma a generation or two earlier were very much without structure or power in their adopted homelands. All tribal people who lived during this era and in this place suffered the effects of external and internal racism. Our family, like many others, didn't escape without deep injuries, emotional, psychological, and physical. My dad wanted a **many** when he married my mom; my mom wanted a stable, trustworthy, and honorable life. Trouble had been too regular a visitor at her young door. Both of my parents put a premium on education and found in each other a way to learn and grow a family together.

Together they built a small army of church-going, instrument-playing, bright-futured children who excelled at many things. We spent the majority of our time in and around church activities. When there were no volunteers for the jobs that needed doing, we were employed (and by employed I mean put to work rather than compensated) to set up for a service, make phone calls, lick envelopes, and run off thousands of copies late into the night. We also used our musical skills (and some had more than others) to accompany a variety of different services in a variety of locations. I vividly remember my dad's folding field organ. It was military issue and could be set up and played in any spot. We powered it by wildly pumping pedals with our feet. It took a real talent to pump and play at the same time. Fortunately, we could all sing so we often used our voices when our hands, feet, and instruments gave out.

Our family also spent a great deal of time around the meal table, often ending the meal with Bible study and hymn singing. As a teenager, I was embarrassed by our ritual. Most of my friends' parents were out of the house when their kids were eating dinner, leaving their kids to fend for themselves. Not us. We were tied together as a family. We did chores and lived a common life whether we wanted to or not. We were a small branch of a larger tribe wandering the world together, serving God and community (some more reluctantly than others), and struggling to find our personal identities in the space between us. We were five kids stuck together in the back of an aging Chrysler along with dog hair, a covered dish, and flowers all crunched against our Sunday finest.

Some of us chose to move as far away from organized religion as possible as we became adults. I did not want to be identified with the church and sought more creative and expressive endeavors I considered counter-cultural and defiant. I wanted to find my way in the world as an independent, self-realized individual. At some point, most of us seek a way to differentiate from our families of origin. We want to explore who we are separate from the pack. As youthful explorers, we can be delusional and idealistic, losing sight of the generations of people who helped to form our particular lens on the world no matter how far we stray from our family. We are defined, at least in part, by the rich cultural soup in which we were raised. The best work we can do, then, is to acknowledge the blessings and curses of our people and find new, authentic ways to define and redefine our relationship with both our family and God. We are embedded in both culture and family. No matter how loosely or tightly wound each is, they help to shape our personalities, our gifts and skills, and our understanding of God. Even as I pushed away, it was through my family of origin that I found my way back to God.

My Cherokee tradition taught me in very different ways to respect all of life. My mother tried to get away from her past and so initially tried to keep us from our Cherokee traditions. We had to pry much of who we are out of her, since she grew up in an era when folks were not particularly proud to be "Indian." Being a faithful Christian meant my mother had been instructed that her cultural past was sinful and of the devil. She knew better, but lived and struggled with the internal conflict. Hence, it took us children pressing and a change in the overall view of society in the past thirty years to have my mother share her true traditional self with us. It is only in recent years that she gave us our Indian names.

Historically, the Cherokee people attempt to keep sacred objects and times separated from other things. We wrap sacred items in deerskin or white cloth when not in use and keep them in a special place. We acknowledge the circle as a symbol with spiritual importance: our Stomp Dance is done in a circle; in former times the fire in the council house was built by arranging the wood in a continuous "X" so that it would burn in a circular path. The "Long Man" or river was considered sacred. We went to the water for purification, healing, and other ceremonies. Still today, any other body of moving water is considered a sacred site. Going to water is still a respected practice by some Cherokees. The spiritual beings in our everyday Cherokee world are considered different from people and animals, but not considered "supernatural." They are very much a part of the natural, real world.

Families of Origin

The strains of living as a family in this day and age are complicated and difficult. The pressures of poverty and illness can tear the best families apart—and that is when there is no mental illness, no drug or alcohol addictions, and no pathologies or abuse in the extended family. Mental illness, addictions, and abuse are also destructive forces. Families can be cruel and dangerous places, and homes are often places of violence rather than refuge. There are no perfect families anywhere and, for better or for worse, we learn about God with people that raise us.

I want to look honestly at our families and the scriptures, not shying from the ugliness, but looking for a deeper understanding of God in the midst of our families, who can be the worst demonstrations of humanity as well as incubators of love and grace. I hope to help us all find God right where we are, rather than in some storybook theme park fantasy of either God or family. We are bound together, no matter how far we scatter ourselves. God still has good news for us in the here and now, despite the traumas and calamities we face.

Methodology

In each chapter, I will offer several stories from sibling and family relationships taken from the Bible. Many will be familiar to the reader and some will be less so. I am using the *New Revised Standard Version* of the Bible for the texts that are quoted in each chapter.

I will offer my responses and insights to these passages and relate stories from my own life and travels that resonate with the themes articulated in each story. The book is also peppered with poems I have written over the years in response to certain stories from the Bible and in the midst of certain seasons of my life. I wish I could include photos, video, and music as well, since I believe that our creative expressions, however feeble the attempts might seem, help us enter into the stream of creation, into the bloodstream of a living God. At the end of each chapter are questions to help elicit connections between the reader and the stories. I consider our faith to be most alive when practiced in community, so these exercises are designed to encourage honesty, laughter, and insight to draw out from individuals and groups both a healthy curiosity and an abundance of creativity. God dwells in our curiosity and creativity, our laughter, and our common concern.

I also offer stories and explanations from my people, the Cherokees. Understanding and participating in the tribal ceremonies and customs shaped who I am as a person, as a mother, grandmother, and as a Bishop. The ancient traditions still run deep in my family. The inclusion of Cherokee traditions is also an invitation to the reader to include the ceremonies, traditions, and insights of his or her own ancestors. The ancestral heritage of many Americans has been submerged in an over-arching culture that often subsumes uniqueness into the great "mixing bowl." No matter how we try not to be, we are all still people of unique racial, cultural, and religious histories. We are invited to explore the depth and richness of our ancestors in order to know God in both new and ancient ways.

Take Heart

I have been lying here so long burnt
by the sun and rain soaked waiting
to put my legs under me and run.

When I dream feet and legs fly
through forest winged fast night running
I am movement and fearless.

Waking I see the sorrow in your eyes shaded
lifting me from this stained palate washing
away grim and foul dark emissions dependent
on other I smile silently weeping.

I am broken yes not dead others
pass by afraid to look fearing becoming
frozen to the bed like me.

I ache to be touched
told a story
sung a song.

I wish to hold you
tell you my dreams
and sing you my secrets.

I am more that this shattered pot this
saggy wreck of a structure grace and
balance still within me rattle around
looking for a foothold.

You look at me and know tender
and broken I am fiercely strong
my heart jealous of the movers legs
I covet muscle I would steal.

You come and touch forgiving my angry
heart made whole sensation returned
tears cascade for life is returning
I have no voice but my feet sing your song.

based on *Matthew* 9:1–3

Naked and Confused:
Bad Parenting 101

Each family and each individual, just like every religion, has a creation myth, a story of beginning that defines the culture and the context of who we are. In this chapter, we listen again to the stories of our faith that have fashioned how we think of God and our place in the cosmos while reflecting on what these stories might say about our relationships inside of the family and in the larger faith community.

Imagine a family gathered around a table at the holidays. Someone will inevitably bring up a story from the past by saying, "I'll never forget the time when—" and then go on to tell something embarrassing or traumatic (or possibly both). These are the creation stories of the clan. The stories have in themselves the makings of a myth, if they have not already become so. They tell of how a people were formed or reformed, in reaction to or because of some event. In these decisive events, we may choose to find the hand of God working behind the scenes. The stories get bigger with each telling, and have to be retold at certain kinds of huge events: baptisms, weddings, and funerals. We might not like them, and might cringe with embarrassment and revulsion, but they are critical to understanding our theology and our relationship to God.

Robert Coles writes in his book *The Spiritual Life of Children*,

the child's racial background, religious background, even socioeconomic background, and the child's personal life definitely influenced the way the child thinks of God and will picture God. Christian children were very anxious to draw pictures of Jesus and, indeed, of God. There was a great deal of variation depending on where they lived and what their neighborhood was like and who they usually see and therefore what colors come naturally to them as they pick up their pencils and the crayons and the paints." [2]

Our theology—our God story—is embedded in our creation, culture, and family stories. We cannot help but paint God from our experience, coloring God with the language we have learned from our families and communities.

Adam and Eve—A Garden of Expulsion

They heard the sound of the Lord God walking in the garden at the time of the evening breeze, and the man and his wife hid themselves from the presence of the Lord God among the trees of the garden. But the Lord God called to the man, and said to him, "Where are you?" He said, "I heard the sound of you in the garden, and I was afraid, because I was naked; and I hid myself." He said, "Who told you that you were naked? Have you eaten from the tree of which I commanded you not to eat?" The man said, "The woman whom you gave to be with me, she gave me fruit from the tree, and I ate." Then the Lord God said to the woman, "What is this that you have done?" The woman said, "The serpent tricked me, and I ate." The Lord God said to the serpent, "Because you have done this, cursed

---

[2] Boston: Houghton Mifflin, 1990, 146.

are you among all animals and among all wild creatures; upon your belly you shall go, and dust you shall eat all the days of your life. I will put enmity between you and the woman, and between your offspring and hers; he will strike your head, and you will strike his heel." To the woman he said, "I will greatly increase your pangs in childbearing; in pain you shall bring forth children, yet your desire shall be for your husband, and he shall rule over you." And to the man he said, "Because you have listened to the voice of your wife, and have eaten of the tree about which I commanded you, 'You shall not eat of it,' cursed is the ground because of you; in toil you shall eat of it all the days of your life; thorns and thistles it shall bring forth for you; and you shall eat the plants of the field. By the sweat of your face you shall eat bread until you return to the ground, for out of it you were taken; you are dust, and to dust you shall return." The man named his wife Eve, because she was the mother of all who live. And the Lord God made garments of skins for the man and for his wife, and clothed them.

Then the Lord God said, "See, the man has become like one of us, knowing good and evil; and now, he might reach out his hand and take also from the tree of life, and eat, and live for ever"—therefore the Lord God sent him forth from the garden of Eden, to till the ground from which he was taken. He drove out the man; and at the east of the Garden of Eden he placed the cherubim, and a sword flaming and turning to guard the way to the tree of life. (Genesis 3:8–24)

As I see it, Eve was just trying to feed her husband something exotic. He had been complaining to her for days that he was tired of her dinners. Adam thought that in this perfect garden, every meal should be perfect, although he was as adventurous as he had originally led her to believe. She had no other men for comparison, yet she still found herself wishing for more from him. The guava was giving him gas and the starch and beans were making his belly swell. She thought it might be that he didn't move around so much as he used to, and had gotten a little too comfortable in the small dwelling they had fashioned in the garden. Wandering around, pushing her cart through the Eden grocery aisles, she heard the sweet whisper of a charming, dazzling green snake. Desperate for some help, she talked back to the snake. Yeah, she should have left well enough alone, but life is complicated, even when you are the only two people in a perfect garden.

Everybody is in need of a little excitement now and then—even the perfectly formed, completely pampered, and privileged. Adam couldn't help that he had a short attention span. Eve was made with a good measure of curiosity, which she couldn't seem to do anything with in a place where everything and everyone was completely cared for and well manicured. Mister Excitement Adam wasn't, and she was just trying to put some excitement in their lives, even if she didn't really know what that was. Heck, it took messing up and eating the apple for God to give these two real names and the desire to procreate. Things in the garden might have been considerably more exciting if God had given them names and some idea what to do with each other. As a parent-creator, the Lord Almighty might have been more attentive to his instructional and teaching duties. They wanted to understand who they were and how to celebrate that. Up until the apple debacle, they were getting little or no instruction, or at least there is no indication from the text about any teaching. Adam was to control the beasts he named, and armed with God-given creativity, it was only a matter of time before experimenting began. Along comes a snake offering a way to understand and experience excitement, and to share some of that excitement and creativity with her husband. What women wouldn't jump at the chance?

Life had gotten a little too predictable and that was making Eve itchy all over. Or it might have been those pretty leaves she sat in the other day when she was trying to avoid listening to Adam talk again about the rams and the eagles. She liked the more exotic creatures in the garden, the peacock and the slow lorus, the lotus blossoms and the magpies. Adam was so predictable. He liked the most aggressive fighters, the noblest beasts. Sometimes he was a beast but when Eve tried to talk to God about it, all she heard in reply was that all of creation took time and matured at different rates. Some solace for a woman whose only other companion seemed like the one with delayed development. A desire to understand became the impetus to reach beyond the safe, to stretch into the outer limits of her cognition. A bite from the fruit and she understood: they were fully human with all the flaws and desires indicative of humanity. God sat down at the sewing machine and crafted, created covering since they understood who they were and sent them away to make babies. They had to have names, like all children, and deal with the bumps and scrapes of life. In sending them away from the perfect, sheltered garden, God promised that their lives would be a living hell, at times, something they hadn't experienced in the garden, where they neither had real want nor real choice.

We all have our garden expulsion stories. There are moments in each of our lives that we figure some things out and think we understand everything and we know it all. Shortly thereafter we hit the wall and realize how dependent we are, how sorely we need each other, and how much we rely on God's help. Sometimes it happens when the money runs out, or when the good clothes that were always kept clean for us finally wear out and smell so bad that we are ashamed to be seen in them. Whatever it is, we find ourselves outside the garden, beginning to understand who we are, learning our names, and crying like babies to go home again, back to the garden where we were safe.

Parents of young adults often struggle as their children become competent adults and seek the freedom of life on their own. The young adults really believe their parents to be less than competent and the parents think likewise of their offspring. Expulsion from the garden might ring familiar to those young adults who were too smart for their own good and got sent away from home, to fend for themselves. Many a parent prays that their children will be fine as they send them away, and hope the child's life is enough of a challenge, a good stiff sip of hellfire, that the child will finally appreciate the tender loving care given them and what that tender care really cost the parents. Gray hairs are the least of the cost of rearing children.

When I was expecting our first child, I was young and certain that I knew so much more about raising children than my parents did. It was the late 1970s, and natural childbirth and rearing were dominating the scene. My parents were not bohemian and alternative like we were, and they stifled us with their rules and regulations, or so it seemed at the time. I was fervent, and sure that I would take everything in stride and show my mom and dad a thing or two. After Emily was born, healthy and lively, my parents came for a brief visit to see their first granddaughter. It was a nice day and we had a wonderful time. My mother reluctantly got in the car for a long ride home with my dad. She offered to stay, but I was confident that I was so good at parenting that nothing could undo me.

Less than two weeks later, standing in the kitchen barefoot and dirty, short on sleep and with a colicky baby in my arms, I gave in and called my mother. I sobbed my eyes out and told her I was ruining everything. I thought I was a horrible mother and this beautiful child didn't deserve me. I continued to cry until it was all out. She asked me if she could come and help me and I jumped at the chance. It was then she told me that she had a bag in the back of the car that day of the visit, packed and ready to stay if I had asked. She loved me enough to know if I didn't ask she wouldn't force herself on me.

My mother came on the next available train and helped me with all my messes until I was confident and rested. Over and over again she interjected herself into my life as I needed. My children are safe and alive because she came to my rescue. All I needed to do was ask. I was never afraid to ask again. God, standing in the cool of the morning in that Garden, looked on his creation and knew how hard they would struggle and how they would have to find their way back. The Creator had a suitcase packed ready to be with them, ready to help them through their messes until they could stand on their own two feet, but they sure took a long time in asking. Adam and Eve, the first two human parents, the ones who had been so fortunate to live in the perfect Garden, began creating a family with great expectations. Where they ended up was so different from what they expected. Though they left a great legacy, they also left a great mess.

Little Ones

Slumbering the night air moving trees
dreams slide through the quiet startling me
awake with fear for my little ones.

Did I hear a cry in the night rising
slowing approaching heart fluttering bravery
lost to concern for these little ones.

Daylight and they wander off brave
with no brains or fear as yet darkness
settles and our nightmares begin.

I creep to the crib and all is safe breathing
lifts the sweet small chest and the breath
of an angel sour milk and freedom dreams
permeates the air.

I awake to know the heart of God beating
within mine aching to protect and shield
harboring the little ones
from those who would snatch and destroy.

Tonight the little ones are nestled warm
and snug in the heart of God and known in
a mother's trembling heart and grateful sigh.

based on *Matthew* 18:10–14

Raising Cain and Abel

Now the man knew his wife Eve, and she conceived and bore Cain, saying, "I have produced a man with the help of the Lord." Next she bore his brother Abel. Now Abel was a keeper of sheep, and Cain a tiller of the ground. In the course of time Cain brought to the Lord an offering of the fruit of the ground, and Abel for his part brought of the firstlings of his flock, their fat portions. And the Lord had regard for Abel and his offering, but for Cain and his offering he had no regard. So Cain was very angry, and his countenance fell. The Lord said to Cain, "Why are you angry, and why has your countenance fallen? If you do well, will you not be accepted? And if you do not do well, sin is lurking at the door; its desire is for you, but you must master it."

Cain said to his brother Abel, "Let us go out to the field." And when they were in the field, Cain rose up against his brother Abel and killed him. Then the Lord said to Cain, "Where is your brother Abel?" He said, "I do not know; am I my brother's keeper?" And the Lord said, "What have you done? Listen; your brother's blood is crying out to me from the ground! And now you are cursed from the ground, which has opened its mouth to receive your brother's blood from your hand. When you till the ground, it will no longer yield to you its strength; you will be a fugitive and a wanderer on the earth." Cain said to the Lord, "My punishment is greater than I can bear! Today you have driven me away from the soil, and I shall be hidden from your face; I shall be a fugitive and a wanderer on the earth, and anyone who meets me may kill me." Then the Lord said to him, "Not so! Whoever kills Cain will suffer a sevenfold vengeance." And the Lord put a mark on Cain, so that no one who came upon him would kill him. Then Cain went away from the presence of the Lord, and settled in the land of Nod, east of Eden. (Genesis 4:1–16)

We don't get a lot of information from this Genesis story about how Adam and Eve fared in setting up household or how often they went to God for help and support. Somehow it seems they were not far off from the Garden and the Creator who was keeping an eye on them, making sure they were safe and sound, despite themselves. The story gives evidence of the close relationship of God to the first family, with the naming of Cain (made with God's help) and the expectation that the young men would make an offering to God and God would respond to them personally. They were just a little bit removed from the Garden and had enough food and shelter to get by. There were crops in the field and sheep in the meadow. They were a simple family, but well provisioned with a direct connection to God. We don't hear much about Eve in this story. We can only imagine she spent a good deal of time screaming in labor and screaming at the snakes that hid in her garden. I am sure she had some regular words with God on many subjects, but the compilers of Genesis thought those were best left out.

Eve must have wept bitterly after her younger son was killed by his older brother. She must have had some harsh words for God in those dark, painful days and months. God had accepted Abel's offering and shunned Cain's. The brilliant Creative Force behind the universe and life itself had refused to honor Cain's offering. It must have been a nightmare for Eve and Adam, for God to give them these beautiful and strong sons, only to have one taken away by violence and the other expelled to the land East of Eden. He was sent to a place where there were others who would murder him in a minute, a place of trouble and distrust, where God didn't talk to the locals on any sort of regular basis. The first man and woman had to abide with their expulsion, the depths of loss and the expulsion of their son to another community altogether, and a community who didn't know God or their days in the garden.

Their expulsion and loss had begun with the curious human behavior of self-discovery. They were disobedient and tasted the forbidden fruit, but they also were intelligent enough to know what they had done and to hide themselves. Their simple, idyllic lives were crushed by their own curiosity and the punishment their Creator had for the newly minted creation. All along, they kept in relationship to the Creator, talking with, walking with, and offering the first fruits of their labors to the God of their existence. Then things went horribly wrong and it seemed so easy to blame God for their loss. If God was so perfect and all-knowing, how come this disaster wasn't prevented? Did God not love them enough, or were they so awful a creation that they were being rejected? The children seemed set to be the victims of bad parenting and confusion over roles with the Creator and in their struggle to find out who they are in the midst of their known universe. Just when they thought things had been figured out, they were hit with unbearable tragedy.

Call me Ishmael

Now Sarai, Abram's wife, bore him no children. She had an Egyptian slave-girl whose name was Hagar, and Sarai said to Abram, "You see that the Lord has prevented me from bearing children; go in to my slave-girl; it may be that I shall obtain children by her." And Abram listened to the voice of Sarai. So, after Abram had lived for ten years in the land of Canaan, Sarai, Abram's wife, took Hagar the Egyptian, her slave-girl, and gave her to her husband Abram as a wife. He went in to Hagar, and she conceived; and when she saw that she had conceived, she looked with contempt on her mistress. Then Sarai said to Abram, "May the wrong done to me be on you! I gave my slave-girl to your embrace, and when she saw that she had conceived, she looked on me with contempt. May the Lord judge between you and me!" But Abram said to Sarai, "Your slave-girl is in your power; do to her as you please." Then Sarai dealt harshly with her, and she ran away from her.

The angel of the Lord found her by a spring of water in the wilderness, the spring on the way to Shur. And he said, "Hagar, slave-girl of Sarai, where have you come from and where are you going?" She said, "I am running away from my mistress Sarai." The angel of the Lord said to her, "Return to your mistress, and submit to her." The angel of the Lord also said to her, "I will so greatly multiply your offspring that they cannot be counted for multitude." And the angel of the Lord said to her, "Now you have conceived and shall bear a son; you shall call him Ishmael, for the Lord has given heed to your affliction. He shall be a wild ass of a man, with his hand against everyone, and everyone's hand against him; and he shall live at odds with all his kin." So she named the Lord who spoke to her, "You are El-roi"; for she said, "Have I really seen God and remained alive after seeing him?" Therefore the well was called Beer-lahai-roi; it lies between Kadesh and Bered.

Hagar bore Abram a son; and Abram named his son, whom Hagar bore, Ishmael. Abram was eighty-six years old when Hagar bore him Ishmael. (Genesis 16:1–16)

Just when you think that the Creator and all related human beings are finding ways to cope with the basics, we come across the story of Hagar and the son she has with Abram: Ishmael. This poor woman and her kid couldn't get a break. Hagar's owner, old Sarai, wanted a baby real bad, and women can be extraordinarily persistent when it comes to wanting a child. A normally rational woman can become unglued. The normal relations with her husband weren't working, the biology was against her with her age, and her fears for her future and leaving no legacy were coming to a boil. Scheming night and day, she finally offered her young slave girl Hagar to the old man, and voila—Hagar conceived. Sarai was furious, even though it had been her plan. She was riddled with jealousy and guilt, and in her anger nearly beat the girl to death. Bleeding from her wounds, and sobbing inconsolably, Hagar left the protective care of her awful owner and took off into the desert to die. At least she wouldn't be beaten night and day and called a whore. Her aching body and swollen belly made her journey horrific and she fell down in her tears waiting for the end and her release from bondage.

Hagar was greeted by an angel, as God was listening nearby and ached for her and the state of things. The angel promised her good care if she returned to Sarai and Abram, and told her she would be the mother of a great nation. I imagine Hagar did not care to be a great matriarch; she just wanted to get away from the crazy old people. But she listened to the angel and she returned to the house of her owners to find the air had cleared and the tension had died down. She sat at the edge of the tent, her belly getting rounder every day, wondering exactly what God was up to. Did the angel really say her son would be a wild ass of a man and be at war with his family? Did returning to the fold mean living with the promise of strife and wrestling all of her life? She took comfort in the knowledge that God had sought her out in the desert, that she was given water and food, that she was cared for, and—whatever she faced— she could hold that moment in her mind and know that God was nearby listening to her heartfelt cries. Somehow, despite the fact that she was just property, she was honored by God and bore the first child to Abram, the father of the Judeo-Christian and Muslim world, the grand forebearer of all stories that proceed thereafter. She is a mother of the faith, despite her rejection and her life's burdens; she was found by God and never left alone again.

Old Enough to Know Better than to Laugh at God

The Lord appeared to Abraham by the oaks of Mamre, as he sat at the entrance of his tent in the heat of the day. He looked up and saw three men standing near him. When he saw them, he ran from the tent entrance to meet them, and bowed down to the ground. He said, "My lord, if I find favor with you, do not pass by your servant. Let a little water be brought, and wash your feet, and rest yourselves under the tree. Let me bring a little bread, that you may refresh yourselves, and after that you may pass on—since you have come to your servant." So they said, "Do as you have said." And Abraham hastened into the tent to Sarah, and said, "Make ready quickly three measures of choice flour, knead it, and make cakes." Abraham ran to the herd, and took a calf, tender and good, and gave it to the servant, who hastened to prepare it. Then he took curds and milk and the calf that he had prepared, and set it before them; and he stood by them under the tree while they ate.

They said to him, "Where is your wife Sarah?" And he said, "There, in the tent." Then one said, "I will surely return to you in due season, and your wife Sarah shall have a son." And Sarah was listening at the tent entrance behind him. Now Abraham and Sarah were old, advanced in age; it had ceased to be with Sarah after the manner of women. So Sarah laughed to herself, saying, "After I have grown old, and my husband is old, shall I have pleasure?" The Lord said to Abraham, "Why did Sarah laugh, and say, "Shall I indeed bear a child, now that I am old?" Is anything too wonderful for the Lord? At the set time I will return to you, in due season, and Sarah shall have a son." But Sarah denied, saying, "I did not laugh'; for she was afraid. He said, "Oh yes, you did laugh." (Genesis 18:1–15)

Throughout history, especially that recorded in the scriptures, men have acted as the authorities on God and religion. The image of God comes to us in form of a man, and the first human creation was male, according to Genesis. Yet we have in this story a moment when the full personhood and understanding of women faces off directly against the authority of man and God. Sarah laughs. Most women I know who are of a vintage beyond childrearing are glad to be done with that time of their lives. From young girlhood, women are faced with monthly physical and emotional disturbances. In the history of many traditional cultures, women moved away from their families and especially the men during their menses to a separate dwelling, a separate tent. For modern women, despite the many scientific and pharmaceutical innovations, that time of the month is still a challenge and never glorious. Modern men might also wish that some of the women they love, live, and work with might move themselves away for that time. We women know how the hormones change the way we interact with others and how we look at the world. Some are bothered only a little by their monthly flow and others suffer greatly. A friend of mine recently remarked that if men had to monthly go through what we do, there would be a new design for how babies are brought into the world. Women, who bear the pain of childbirth and carry the growing child within them for nine months, are incarnationally aware of the biology of birth and the reality of children. Sarah laughed, most probably because she was afraid, and maybe—just maybe—because she thought her husband had gone too far and had become an over-the-edge religious zealot. I, too, find myself laughing when scared and uncomfortable and when it seems as if God has put me in an untenable position with folks who seem to want to volunteer me for a duty and calling beyond my known capacity.

Sarah found herself in an untenable situation. God had talked to her husband directly, but not to her. She had to listen in, to eavesdrop as it were, on the conversation. She was afraid because, in all the years she was married, she had failed at producing a child. The one role she was intended for she was not able to fulfill. She had already struggled with jealousy and rage at the other women who surrounded her husband and seemed to pop out his offspring on an annual basis as if they were fecund ewes dropping new lambs in the field.

Sarah was old and way beyond that time of her life. Her body hurt with age. She no longer wanted to deal with the prospect of another in her body. She was done. She walked stooped over and the thought of carrying another human being around seemed overwhelming. Yet

God made the miracle happen and Sarah bore the pain along with the anxiety and responsibility that all women bear who carry a child to term. All sorts of things could go wrong with a crone being pregnant, let alone giving birth. She had, no doubt, witnessed hundreds of births and seen some beloved family members and friends die in childbirth; she had no idea how she would survive. She was scared, perhaps even slightly hysterical. God was laying the whole burden on her. She had failed for so long that she couldn't see how it would work. She had put motherhood completely behind her and left it to the servant girls. Now, to her shame, fear, and revulsion, God was giving her what she had longed for. She laughed and melted into tears.

"Be careful what you ask God for" is a common phrase in my family. You don't ask my mother to pray for something and not expect it to come about. Many people consider her a very faithful and holy woman, which she is. She is also my mother, and a matriarch in the true Cherokee fashion: very proud and sure of herself. In recent years her memory has become less than it once was, so I often advise people to write down what they want her to pray for. No use confusing God in our prayers or God having to answer some scrambled signal of the proud and holy.

In many traditions is a great honor to name a child. For Cherokees this is an especially honorable task and one that is taken very seriously. We read in the Cherokee Historical Records from Tahlequah, Oklahoma that in 1725 Alexander Longe reported: "The maternal grandmother named daughters and a senior male in the father's lineage named sons." Today it is common for the maternal grandmother to name all her grandchildren with their Cherokee names. Cherokee names are not the same as those given in English, and many times are not even similar in meaning to one another when translated.

My mother waited until she was a grandmother to give me my Cherokee name. Despite the fact that I was named Carol Joy after an aunt, and since I was born on Christmas Eve, my mother named me Waterfalls or *A-ma-ga-lo-s-ga*. It is a very fitting name, as I am most comfortable in the water.

One Basket Case: Moses

Now a man from the house of Levi went and married a Levite woman. The woman conceived and bore a son; and when she saw that he was a fine baby, she hid him for three months. When she could hide him no longer she got a papyrus basket for him, and plastered it with bitumen and pitch; she put the child in it and placed it among the reeds on the bank of the river. His sister stood at a distance, to see what would happen to him.

The daughter of Pharaoh came down to bathe at the river, while her attendants walked beside the river. She saw the basket among the reeds and sent her maid to bring it. When she opened it, she saw the child. He was crying, and she took pity on him. "This must be one of the Hebrews' children," she said. Then his sister said to Pharaoh's daughter, "Shall I go and get you a nurse from the Hebrew women to nurse the child for you?" Pharaoh's daughter said to her, "Yes." So the girl went and called the child's mother. Pharaoh's daughter said to her, "Take this child and nurse it for me, and I will give you your wages." So the woman took the child and nursed it. When the child grew up, she brought him to Pharaoh's daughter, and she took him as her son. She named him Moses, "because," she said, "I drew him out of the water." (Exodus 2:1–10)

In the ancient Middle East, stories of extraordinary birth were essential, if you were an important cultural or religious figure, or especially if you were considered a god, or somehow closely related to God. We hear this story of the infant Moses, however, not as an extraordinary birth story, but as a story of survival. From Jewish tradition, we learn that his father had named him Chaver while his grandfather called him Avigdor. Some scholars say that Pharaoh's daughter actually named him Minios, which means "drawn out" in Egyptian, and the name Moshe (Moses) was a Hebrew translation of that name. Moses was the one who would lead his people out of bondage in a foreign land. By God's help, he would overcome great adversity to see his people free. Moses would never see them back to their homelands, but he was essential to their freedom and new life.

I want to focus on the mother and child in this tale. Can you imagine her fear as she hid her son? Then, as he grew, she had to set him afloat in a basket, only to watch him scooped up by a spoiled princess, her enemy and captor, and named by another. The baby's mother ended up being his wet nurse and always had to call him by the name that was not his, a foreign and arrogant name, one that signified the luck of the wealthy and powerful. His mother, Yocheved, Levi's daughter, must have smiled as she nursed him, looking on the face of love in her child, while at the same time seething with hate for her circumstances. She must have whispered the stories of her people to Moses, and she must have called him by his real name, the name she had given him moments after her painful labor was done. He was flesh of her flesh, pushed from her body and then torn away by political circumstances too complicated for one child to understand. The young boy child was brought up in luxury and privilege surrounded by servants who looked just like him, who doted on him, and sowed in him the seeds of rebellion and sedition.

I have a dear friend who adopted a child about the time my second oldest, Ariel, was born. Amanda and Ariel grew up together and became lifelong friends. One day, when they were both still young infants, I was driving in the car with my two girls, on the way to see my friend. I had been sick for a while, struggling with a bug and was a bit out of sorts. My oldest Emily began to cry. I asked her what the matter was. She told me that she was worried because I had been sick. The last time we had visited Amanda, she had asked her mom why Amanda's birth mother had given her up. Gently my friend told her that Amanda's birth mother had been very sick and had to give up her baby. Emily was worried that I would have to give away her sister and maybe her also. Even as a five year old, Emily understood the great pain of giving up a child, of a mother's horrible choice. Torn from one another, by illness, poverty, or politics, this choice is never a good one, and always leaves much pain to reconcile.

Moses was brought up in the royal court of Egypt and was saturated in the pervasive anti-semitic environment of his young world. Moses was afforded every privilege of a young royal and could have rested in the arms of wealth and stature, living among the powerful and wealthy all his days. But we know the rest of the story. Somehow he was instilled with an ache to free his people, a compassion for the poor and the powerless, and the drive to break from his surroundings and change the world. Out of his mother's tears, in her whispered stories and ancient songs, a man of God grew up to lead his people from bondage into freedom and a new identity, free of the soul-breaking life of captivity.

I have often wondered if the reported speech impediment, the stutter, which brought about his reliance on Aaron, was not a result of an early seeded conflict in his identity. His natural mother, Yocheved, told him who he really was as she nursed him, and yet his surroundings and servants told him another story. He would have internalized his racism, knowing he didn't belong among the royals and conflicted about feeling more at home with the help, which could make even the strongest person stutter. Most every young person feels like an alien in his or her family. I know I asked, "Who are these people who say they are related to me, and why are they so weird?" But Moses knew a far greater identity crisis. The big questions of "Who am I?" and "Where do I belong?" must have been nearly unanswerable for the young man. It is telling that it took him until he was forty to strike out—literally—and grow into his ultimate calling as leader of his people, the Israelites, the captives who would rebuild a great nation of faith.

CHAPTER 1 • REFLECTION

Exercises and Questions

This would be a good time to start a personal journal, if you don't already have one. Begin by telling your story of origin. You might want to talk to your parents, siblings, and other family members about your life as a newborn and a child. This might not be a possible exercise for some, but the conversations with others are still important. Our creation stories tell us how we come into the world, and hint at the purposes God has for us. You can also put together a small photo album of pictures from your early life.

1. Are there themes that emerge from hearing again these stories of Beginning from the Bible?

2. Are there themes that emerge for your life?

3. What in your own story connects you with these stories, and what alienates you?

4. Are there conflicts, cultural, religious, or familial, that have shaped your life?

Children in Conflict: We Barely Left the Garden

In this chapter we move from our beginnings and creation epics to the other most intimate relations that form us: our siblings. Many psychologists have written extensively about the importance of birth order and gender bias in the developmental process. I want us to examine the biblical narratives that define our relationships with our siblings and how we understand God because of them (or despite them).

Those of us who have grown up in a large family, particularly those who have been smashed in the middle of a big brood, will know that our older siblings taught us what to do and what to avoid. The other kids brought us real insights into surviving in school, on the playground, and especially navigating around our parents. Our faith was fashioned by these blood relatives who both had our backs and were the bane of our existence. Life among blood and non-blood related siblings provides many opportunities as well as many challenges, not the least of which is surviving and thriving while held captive in the back seat of the family car.

Our faith, along with our physical bodies, matures with each passing year, or so we hope. Embedded in our physical beings are the remnants of memory, history, and previous beliefs. This is true for our physical and psychological development as well. Renowned child development psychologist Erik Erikson, in his ground-breaking work *Childhood and Society,* identified the earliest stage of our development as basic trust vs. mistrust which occurs during the infant stage or first year of life. As we become upright and walking, we struggle with our will, exploring our autonomy vs. our shame and doubt. In our toddler years we move on to understanding our purpose through balancing initiative vs. guilt. These stages of development cover the years before school and full outside socialization begin.

Much of my first six years of my life were spent on the back window ledge of our car. It was custom in my family that the littlest one rode in the back window. My Dad had a series of big, old Chryslers. None of these cars would fit the present-day term of a "pre-owned luxury car." They were used and housed those massive V-8 engines he so dearly loved. The vehicle had to fit all six of us, along with the family dog. We had a trailer he also loved to pull when we went on trips and vacations. I was six and a half when my youngest sister Betsy was born, so I was the littlest one for quite some time. She was born the summer after my first grade year. I was reading and writing by the time I stopped being the baby of the family. My first vantage point of the world was from that back window ledge. I actually liked it there but most of my view was receding scenery—not where we were going but where we had just been. The shelf was long and narrow, and I loved to lay there watching the road, sometimes reading, sometimes sleeping or singing to myself as the world went fading away, out of my grasp.

The development and intersection of our individuation and autonomy, which occurs during the first six years of life, not only helps defines how we interact socially with our peers, but also how we engage the world on both a personal and cosmic scale. Our early formation, as we struggle with our place in the family and our identity, also sets the stage for how we engage our faith and our understanding of God. We are programmed both by our DNA towards a personality and by our environment for how we engage our exterior and interior lives. I was born smack-dab in the middle of the 1950s, when cars ruled the road, and the road meant everything wonderful about America, and spent six-plus years riding above the heads of my siblings, sometimes kicking them in the head (by accident of course), and on an eye level with my parents who were up front and in control. One can only imagine, as I strap our brand-new grand-daughter into her back-facing, highly evolved car seat, what the next few generations will remember as the cultural context of their very young years.

Daughters Forgive Your Mother

I slept in the rear window
images of trees and where we'd just come from
careened over my sweaty brow
not reflected but absorbed.

Slung between seats and fed by rocking
rhythms from V-8 engine and whining radios
made my home a road through prairies,
over rivers by bowery street.

Impressed by going,
coming of age and leaving
packing bags and rolling out
I am the child of transit on the threshold of a life.
I am the child of motion and flight
born in full season but far away
the home impressed upon my dreams is
fluid motion returning, spinning,
a dance of drumming and becoming.

So I gave birth to spirits and sprites
only at home in dreaming, wind carried songs,
and butterfly wings.
Let go and fly my daughters, for we don't belong here
behind locked doors, no safe house for yearning souls.

The other major cultural influence in my life during those first years of life was the church. My dad was the pastor of the same church for twenty-eight years. My older siblings grew up in several places and lived on military bases. I arrived at six months old, after a cross-country trip hanging from a handmade hammock strung between the seats, to find my place in the pews and hallways of Harrison Presbyterian Church. I can still feel the rigid, biting itch of the crinoline underskirt that made my church dress stick out as I sat in one of the front pews with my mother, brother, and sisters. We took up a whole pew, the five of us, as we looked up every Sunday morning at my dad. The back of the pew in front of us always fascinated me with its little rubber coated cup holders and the wooden slats that held the bibles and hymnals. I liked rearranging the books, flipping the pages—again sometimes singing to myself (not so quietly), trying to read or, at my most bold, stretching out under the pew for a nap. My mother rarely let us get away with anything, so we had to position ourselves out of the reach of her arm. Her look could kill (it was called her black Indian look) and yet, somehow she could manage to smile at my dad and look beatific at the same time.

The town where we lived was, at the time, one of the wealthiest towns in one of the wealthiest counties in the country. It still is a very wealthy community and, though slightly more diverse than it once was, it still boasts a famous country club and homes that sell for stratospheric sums. We were poor by local standards, so living in a posh neighborhood provided a plethora of identity and social conflicts. Our neighbors all had servants and we were friends with the servants' kids as well as the neighbors. The working class folks lived closer to downtown where the church was, and the privileged class had their children delivered to and from public school by their help. As a young native kid, I knew from an early age that this was not my home and these were not my people.

As all young people do, I desperately wanted to fit in, wanted these to be my people, and wanted to think I knew if I dug deep enough among the pretense and the style, I could find my way to God. What I didn't recognize as a child was that some adults around me worshipped other gods: money, power, and prestige. It takes many of us a lifetime to understand that God's desire for us is to have a relationship with our complete and authentic selves. Biblical stories, the culture we are brought up in, and our families of origin can unintentionally encourage us to suppress who we are both in our personal development and our relationship with God. My children have often referred to this posture as the "smile and nod" function, where one keeps his or her true self down to keep the peace. However, God desires more from us than playing a role. We are invited by a loving Creator to find our place and voice in the theology of our person and our community.

The identity of the Cherokee people is rooted in the clan system. The following is taken from a manuscript prepared by J. P. Evans in 1835:

There are no natural boundaries to their clans; the subjects of different clans being mingled. Those of the same clan are considered as belonging to the same family. In fact this relationship seems to be as binding as the ties of consanguinity. An Indian can tell you without hesitating what degree of relationship exists between himself and any other individual of the same clan you may see proper to point out. A man and woman of the same clan are not allowed to become man and wife. This appearance of ancient custom is yet prevalent to some extent, and the disregard of it disgusting in the eyes of many.[3]

Cherokee society is historically matrilineal; meaning clanship comes from the mother. There are seven clans in Cherokee Society: **a ni gi lo hi** (Long Hair), **a ni sa ho ni** (Blue), **a ni wa ya** (Wolf), **a ni go te ge wi** (Wild Potato), **a ni a wi** (Deer), **a ni tsi**

---

[3] From the Cherokee Nation Cultural Resource Center Archives. Available at the museum and online at www.cherokee.org/AboutTheNation/Culture/General/24411/Information.aspx.

s qua (Bird), and **a ni wo di** (Paint). My family is descended from the deer and paint clans. When my mother was born in 1923, traditional practices had been outlawed in Oklahoma and many other states, so much of the tradition was practiced underground and behind closed doors. A people who had been very verbose and who reveled in storytelling became silent in order to survive. It means that until very recently it has been almost impossible for some to feel safe enough to tell their children and grandchildren about their true nature, about their clans, and about the people.

Long before we are fully able to find our voice in society and in a faith community, we are hard wired to find our place within the smaller solar system of our family unit, however it is formed. It is with our siblings, if we are blessed to have them, with whom we work out the next stages of our development. The earlier stages of our development are sorted out in relation to our parents, and we find God in the face and activity of those who give us our initial care. A time comes when our perspective has to widen and we look beyond to siblings and other cohorts for the lessons about life and about God. It is in the sand box and the squabble over toys and dessert that we take the next step to develop our place in the cosmos, however small that definition of cosmos still might be. Our nuclear family, however uniquely defined, is the palate on which we finger paint our way to a deeper understanding of our relationship to God. It is a messy, playful, experimental stage in our faith development. It is the improv, the learning lab, the testing space that allows us to spread our wings and understand at a depth not previously achieved. Because we share so much DNA with our siblings, both inherited and situational, we share a prime testing lab for understanding our humanity and God. Simply said, these are the people we can bond with and irritate the fastest.

My mother tells the story of her two older brothers who regularly played tricks on her as a child. She has a trusting personality and her brothers found ways to take advantage of her. One time, they dug a deep pit, like a trapper would use to catch an animal, and covered it with sticks and leaves, and invited my mother for a walk in the woods with them. She fell in and could not get out. Despite her protests, they walked away and went on playing some other game. As she tells it, she was there for a long time until her mother, inquiring where she had gone, forced marched the boys back to the woods, extricated her, and made Sy and Mac fill the hole back in, among other punishments. My mother laughs about it to this day, although another child might have laid in wait, brooding on revenge in all its forms. Uncle Mac is turning ninety this year; my uncle Sy was lost during the Second World War. Today, my mother and Mac (her brother Charles), who are thirteen months apart in age, share everything in long, rambling phone calls. Our siblings test our personalities because they know us so well. They can push all our buttons at once, and are most often the people who will fight to the death for us.

When I was in third grade or so, I had a lunch box I was very proud of. It was plaid with a matching thermos, and it was metal. It wasn't girly, but sturdy and reliable. I loved it as only a third grader could. One day on the way home from school my next door neighbor Stephen said some horrible things about my brother Don, who was three years my senior. He was my torturer growing up, knowing how to get me to do stupid things and to walk into obvious traps. Without thinking, I raised my lunchbox and clunked Stephen on the head. Despite the fact that Don was my torturer, he was my brother, and nobody, but nobody had the right to say something mean about him. When push came to shove, love and protection overcame everything. For the rest of the year, my lunch box carried the outline of Stephen's head permanently bent into it. It was worth it though; I thought at the time, "He'll never say mean things about my brother again." He didn't—and he was always more respectful of me as well.

Joseph and his Snotty Brothers

Now his brothers went to pasture their father's flock near Shechem. And Israel said to Joseph, "Are not your brothers pasturing the flock at Shechem? Come, I will send you to them." He answered, "Here I am." So he said to him, "Go now, see if it is well with your brothers and with the flock; and bring word back to me." So he sent him from the valley of Hebron. He came to Shechem, and a man found him wandering in the fields; the man asked him, "What are you seeking?" "I am seeking my brothers," he said; "tell me, please, where they are pasturing the flock." The man said, "They have gone away, for I heard them say, 'Let us go to Dothan.'" So Joseph went after his brothers, and found them at Dothan. They saw him from a distance, and before he came near to them, they conspired to kill him. They said to one another, "Here comes this dreamer. Come now, let us kill him and throw him into one of the pits; then we shall say that a wild animal has devoured him, and we shall see what will become of his dreams." But when Reuben heard it, he delivered him out of their hands, saying, "Let us not take his life." Reuben said to them, "Shed no blood; throw him into this pit here in the wilderness, but lay no hand on him"—that he might rescue him out of their hand and restore him to his father. So when Joseph came to his brothers, they stripped him of his robe, the long robe with sleeves that he wore; and they took him and threw him into a pit. The pit was empty; there was no water in it.

Then they sat down to eat; and looking up they saw a caravan of Ishmaelites coming from Gilead, with their camels carrying gum, balm, and resin, on their way to carry it down to Egypt. Then Judah said to his brothers, "What profit is there if we kill our brother and conceal his blood? Come, let us sell him to the Ishmaelites, and not lay our hands on him, for he is our brother, our own flesh." And his brothers agreed. When some Midianite traders passed by, they drew Joseph up, lifting him out of the pit, and sold him to the Ishmaelites for twenty pieces of silver. And they took Joseph to Egypt.

When Reuben returned to the pit and saw that Joseph was not in the pit, he tore his clothes. He returned to his brothers, and said, "The boy is gone; and I, where can I turn?" Then they took Joseph's robe, slaughtered a goat, and dipped the robe in the blood. They had the long robe with sleeves taken to their father, and they said, "This we have found; see now whether it is your son's robe or not." He recognized it, and said, "It is my son's robe! A wild animal has devoured him; Joseph is without doubt torn to pieces." Then Jacob tore his garments, and put sackcloth on his loins, and mourned for his son for many days. All his sons and all his daughters sought to comfort him; but he refused to be comforted, and said, "No, I shall go down to Sheol to my son, mourning." Thus his father bewailed him. Meanwhile the Midianites had sold him in Egypt to Potiphar, one of Pharaoh's officials, the captain of the guard. (Genesis 37:12–36)

The story of Joseph and his brothers is what Howard Gardner would call a meta-narrative: a story big enough to encompass a whole community or a whole people. Sibling rivalry is inherent and hard-wired into our beings, and folks who say otherwise are in denial. Joseph had a different mother than these boys, and they knew how fond their dad was of Rachel, Joseph's mom. He was the long-awaited child from the ice queen, the princess of pretty, the one who didn't like to get her hands dirty. Meanwhile, their mother Leah, the less attractive older sister who tricked Dad into marrying her, worked like a dog day and night to please him. He loved his sons—they knew that, but he doted on Joseph and it made the rest of his hard-working brood furious. The kid didn't lift a finger to help, he sat around all day reading, playing music and being waited on by all the women, wives and concubines alike. Joseph lived a charmed life, in the eyes of his brothers.

Joseph's older brothers could put up with a great deal and got their aggression out by working and playing ball. They had no desire to be hanging around camp watching the women work and even worse, listening to their constant chatter. They were men who despite their petty jealousies could delight in the fruits of their labors. They ate well and slept soundly at the end of the day. Well, they did, until that little snot nose Joseph had a ridiculous dream, and Dad gave him that prized coat. Even though they knew that Joseph looked silly in that coat, his hair flowing like a girl, walking like he was a runway model, they could not forgive him for the uppity dream. That little good-for-nothing brother thought he was better than them, and he was so not even a real man. He was useless in the fields, hanging in the tents like a lady, and weak and lazy like no other. They couldn't believe that Dad would fall for such an obvious ploy—sounding spiritual and insightful—when in truth he was just sucking up so he could live the life of leisure. They didn't think their father would fall for that, and yet he did. Hook, line, and sinker. So they had to do something. They just couldn't take it anymore.

The motivation for murder is often jealousy and rage. When someone is murdered, the police always look at the family first, since more often than not it is a family member who commits the crime. Here we have the story of a band of brothers who couldn't stand the inequality in their family. They plotted murder as they sat out in the fields watching the flocks and huddling around the fire. A little liquid courage was probably in the mix as well. They were fed up with the dreamer and his ways. They wrangled and argued until they found a brilliant and profitable way to move forward. Underneath all of the rage, anger, and frustration, they loved their little half-brother, but they found themselves in an untenable position. The family was divided over a parent's love. It would be the love of God and the filial affection that would ultimately heal a nation likewise.

There is no one in the world that is as close, both genetically and emotionally, as a sibling. At the same time, siblings are the people most likely to irritate us, or tease and torture us. They are the ones who taunt us to our faces and do nasty tricks behind our backs. Forced to sit at the kids' table as adults during Thanksgiving, it is often these pranks and petty irritation that get spoken about with great fondness in later years. Yet, when the rage of jealousy turns to inflicting harm, normal developmental changes to pathology.

Sometimes in families, separation and abandonment happen due to circumstances beyond the adults' control, and can cause deep-seated jealousy and confusion in children of any age. Like Joseph, we find ourselves in alien territory, with unknown relatives, in schools and situations that make us particularly vulnerable. That vulnerability can lead to self-doubt and a desire to be restored, even when we had no hand in the separation and are simply collateral damage.

When my mother was about eleven years old, she was put on a bus with thirty-five cents and sent across the country to live with relatives. Initially her brother was to go with her but decided at the last minute, according to her, to stay with the rest of the family. They were to follow months later. The domestic situation was deteriorating rapidly and my grandmother had decided to take the family east to relatives. Oklahoma in the 1930s was caught in the height of both the Dust Bowl and the Depression. My mother tells this story often enough that my daughters call it her "thirty-five cents story." She made dozens of bus connections, eating often at the hand of generous travelers. Her mother had given her very detailed instructions on what to do and how to behave. Fortunately, the driver and other adults took pity on the young Indian girl and made sure she was safe and fed.

On her last day of travel, she was to wash herself all over and put on her best clothes, according to her mother's very specific instructions. She went to the restroom on her final stop and gave herself a careful wash, sliding into her clean but road-weary best clothes. While she was dressing she heard the voice of the driver, calling for her. She was a little girl holding up a bus load of adults and she was frightened that she was in trouble. She wished she wasn't so alone and so afraid. Fortunately, the bus driver understood when she explained her mother's clear instructions. Through her tears she asked for a few more minutes, and they all must have chuckled with compassion and understanding as she struggled into her outfit alone, with tears streaming down her face, and exhaustion and anxiety trembling through her body.

When my mother arrived in Syracuse, she was met with a crowd from the family, neighborhood, and church. Someone even brought a cake because it was such an occasion that this little Cherokee girl was arriving so far from home. She still recounts this story with much emotion and full of memory nearly eighty years later. It was a foundational experience in her life, leading to much wonder and confusion as she grew. There was also some pride in herself and her capacity alongside of the concern as to why she was sent alone and had to live without her mother and siblings for many months alone. The strength and questions all rolled together.

I can only imagine that the questions and concerns rolled around in Joseph's mind as well as he sat in captivity and as he gazed out from his royal living quarters. The actions of adults—his mother and father—along with his brothers, had sent him from home to be abandoned and sold and left on his own to fend for himself. As he dressed himself, staring into a mirror, he must have wondered what his family was up to and where was God in it all. He must have shaken with anxiety and fear as tears rolled down his face. He was a little boy, alone and aching for his home, his bed, and the only family that he knew. He would make a new life, in a new place, and save his people from starvation. But first he was a little lost boy. No one came looking for him. No one followed. As the years went by, he must have asked God, "Why me?" There would always be a challenge to his strength and faith, whenever he remembered the little boy who was shaking in front of the mirror, a long way from home.

Jacob and Esau: Food Fights

These are the descendants of Isaac, Abraham's son: Abraham was the father of Isaac, and Isaac was forty years old when he married Rebekah, daughter of Bethuel the Aramean of Paddan-aram, sister of Laban the Aramean. Isaac prayed to the Lord for his wife, because she was barren; and the Lord granted his prayer, and his wife Rebekah conceived. The children struggled together within her; and she said, "If it is to be this way, why do I live?" So she went to inquire of the Lord. And the Lord said to her, "Two nations are in your womb, and two peoples born of you shall be divided; one shall be stronger than the other, the elder shall serve the younger." When her time to give birth was at hand, there were twins in her womb. The first came out red, all his body like a hairy mantle; so they named him Esau. Afterwards his brother came out, with his hand gripping Esau's heel; so he was named Jacob. Isaac was sixty years old when she bore them. When the boys grew up, Esau was a skilful hunter, a man of the field, while Jacob was a quiet man, living in tents. Isaac loved Esau, because he was fond of game; but Rebekah loved Jacob.

Once when Jacob was cooking a stew, Esau came in from the field, and he was famished. Esau said to Jacob, "Let me eat some of that red stuff, for I am famished!" (Therefore he was called Edom.) Jacob said, "First sell me your birthright." Esau said, "I am about to die; of what use is a birthright to me?" Jacob said, "Swear to me first." So he swore to him, and sold his birthright to Jacob. Then Jacob gave Esau bread and lentil stew, and he ate and drank, and rose and went his way. Thus Esau despised his birthright. (Genesis 25:19–34)

In most any family, no matter how that family is constructed, food is a big issue, especially among the children. It is no surprise, therefore, that we find ourselves gathered around the Table as the central part of our worship, the physical symbols of God's love in this world focused in the bread and wine. As we are fed, so we know God. "They knew him in the breaking of the bread" (Luke 24:29–33). I once had a small child tell me as I was leaning over the rail distributing Communion bread, "I want more Jesus!" We are people that know God at the table. Many families find their common identity at the table, over food and in the common fare of their lives. Cultures and people are also known by their food. Native people, tribe by tribe, have food that says home to us, food that always needs to be present if there is any kind of celebration. Grandmothers teach their grandchildren how to make these dishes that define them as the people of the tribe. The food tells the ancient story that ties us in the present to those who carried us in ages past. For the Cherokees, as for many other tribes in North America, corn, beans, and squash play an important role in both the everyday meals and the ceremonial foods of our people and nation. They can be found, along with hickory nuts, turkey, and venison, at most every gathering of the clans.

There are also foods that have become popular and part of what is considered traditional Native foods, meaning they are always found at Pow Wows. Pow Wows are generally intertribal gatherings that include much trading and eating, along with ball playing, grand entries, and much dancing. Many tribes will have their own Pow Wows, but even these quickly become multi-tribal as most of us cannot resist the sound of the drum, nor the smell of the food. Fry bread, a wheat quick bread sometimes made with corn, is something that everyone seeks out at the Pow Wow. A good fry bread maker often has a following. The dough is patted flat and then fried quickly in hot grease—once animal fat, now usually Crisco. We can be competitive when we want to about fry bread. Fry bread defines us, and we see our fry bread as our common currency of food. Although it was not historically traditional in every tribe, it is now imbued with an importance for a large group of people, across many nations.

In the story of Jacob and Esau, twins born totally different from one another, we can find ourselves. They most probably were fraternal twins, rather than identical, being different in both looks and temperament. Esau was a man's man, and their father, Isaac, thought he was terrific. On the other hand, the old man did not understand Jacob at all, as he liked to cook, play music, hang around home, read good books, and have meaningful discussions with his friends. He was useless as a hunter and a laborer, two things that were important to Isaac. Esau worked side by side with his father, sweating and groaning, silently toiling and making a bond that seemed unbreakable and invincible. All of us have a weak spot, and Esau was a man of great appetite and little patience. His physical needs always outweighed the needs of anyone or anything else. He did not think, he acted, and his brother Jacob, who was a good observer of his twin, knew just how vulnerable Esau was when he was hungry. It probably started out small. When they were little tykes, Jacob might have bargained for a prized toy in exchange for part of his food. Jacob knew his mom was a soft touch and she wouldn't let him starve. Jacob knew how to be patient; Esau knew no such thing. Year after year Jacob pushed his brother back over food until finally the drama escalated to the point that Esau gave away his birthright for some tasty lentil stew. This was not a singular event, but the completion of an ongoing challenge for a seconds-younger brother who wanted to see exactly what he could get away with. He won the ultimate prize—at least in his own estimation: control of the future of the family land and livestock, the tents, and the women.

Our daughters still talk about the "I'll give you a dollar" days. When my oldest daughter was still in grade school, she found out she could get her younger sisters to do what she wanted if she offered to pay them. Time and time again they would argue over something until Emily would offer one little one or the other a dollar and they would do her bidding. They never seemed to catch on that she never intended to pay them, nor did they wise up and demand to have the cash before the job was done. My daughter Ariel is convinced that her older sister still owes her a million bucks. I tried to teach them the phrase, "Show me the money," but somehow they still got caught in the trap more often than not. A few dollars did exchange hands, which is probably the reason that the younger girls remained hopeful that the payoff was indeed coming.

The story of Esau and Jacob is the story of the struggle of both children and nations. We see in this story the microcosm and the macrocosm of how closely related people, as twins surely are, can be so different and how those differences can create epic divisions that leave deep scars. We see within our own families how similar and different the children are and how each generation struggles simultaneously for understanding and control. It is also a story of the division of the parents and how divided affection can further drive children apart, and even set the stage for the continuing conflicts and dramas that escalate among siblings in later generations. The relationship of the parents has a direct effect on the children because in that relationship children often find some of their earliest understandings of God. In these twins, these fathers of nations, these progenitors of a religious tradition both ancient and wise, the seeds of division and conflict are embedded in their very early nurture, along with the struggle for power and control. One has to wonder what the domestic struggles were between Isaac and Rebekah that would cause them to openly divide their children against themselves, and what terror these parents had lived through in their childhoods. We know that Isaac was offered to God as a slaughtered animal, a sacrificial lamb, which could have left him, as a small boy, wondering about a God and a father who would be willing to offer up an innocent little boy as a sign of faithfulness. The twins were born into a world of conflict that they could not help but reenact, over and over again. As in many families, the unresolved issues and struggles between parents and previous generations become food for the children.

Sons of Thunders with Egos to Match

James and John, the sons of Zebedee, came forward to him and said to him, "Teacher, we want you to do for us whatever we ask of you." And he said to them, "What is it you want me to do for you?" And they said to him, "Grant us to sit, one at your right hand and one at your left, in your glory." But Jesus said to them, "You do not know what you are asking. Are you able to drink the cup that I drink, or be baptized with the baptism that I am baptized with?" They replied, "We are able." Then Jesus said to them, "The cup that I drink you will drink; and with the baptism with which I am baptized, you will be baptized; but to sit at my right hand or at my left is not mine to grant, but it is for those for whom it has been prepared."

When the ten heard this, they began to be angry with James and John. So Jesus called them and said to them, "You know that among the Gentiles those whom they recognize as their rulers lord it over them, and their great ones are tyrants over them. But it is not so among you; but whoever wishes to become great among you must be your servant, and whoever wishes to be first among you must be slave of all. For the Son of Man came not to be served but to serve, and to give his life a ransom for many." (Mark 10:35–45)

In my mind, it is no surprise that these two handsome, vigorous young men wanted a place of honor. They were the kind of young men who were used to being chosen first. Everybody wanted these guys on their team because they were powerful, strong, and able to make anyone a winner. They may not have been the brightest in the group, but they were the kind of guy every dad wants for their daughter, the kind of son-in-law that might make a mother-in-law swoon. They were strong, polite, handsome, and unflappable; they were deserving of respect by their physical presence alone. Zebedee's two boys were A-list types; they were on every invite list and never understood that their privilege was not something they had earned but a birthright given because of their prowess. They showed their ignorance by assuming it was appropriate to ask for what they felt they deserved.

Years ago, I was newly married and working in the library at

Johns Hopkins University. I was outside taking a lunch break on a perfect spring day in Baltimore after having taken a swim, lingering by the gymnasium so I didn't have to go back to my underground office. As I sat and ate my sandwich, a bus pulled up in the circular drive. The doors opened, and young men started descending into the bright air. They were dressed in khakis and button down shirts, all wearing ties and carrying their lacrosse sticks as if they were royal scepters. In no hurry, they swaggered as they took in their new environment and waited for the bus driver to unload their bags.

It was then I realized they were the opposition for the weekend's lacrosse game. The young men were from Harvard and they all believed themselves to be something special. There was never a doubt in any of them that they should be treated with anything but respect and deference. There was no question in their minds about their importance and prowess. Sadly for them, the Harvard team went down in a dreadful defeat that Saturday. Their assumptions about their rightful place and what they deserved on the field of play might have been undermined a bit by the score, but I would hazard to guess that these young gentlemen never thought about being great by serving others, or by giving up their seat or place to someone not from their rank in society.

The story of the request of James and John is told in a slightly different fashion in Matthew's gospel. It is not James and John who make the request of Jesus, but rather their mother. She asks Jesus to promise to give the best seats in the house to her magnificent offspring. She knows they are truly deserving. She is their mother and can objectively point out what incredible creatures they are, what magnificent men they have grown up to be. I truly wonder why Matthew's later gospel tosses this role to a woman. Did the gospel writer really think that only a mother would ask for this kind of favor? It sheds light on the culture and expectations of the gospel story tellers and the writers and editors alike during the first centuries of Christianity, that they were comfortable having a mother ask a place for her sons. Parents across time have been known to be willing to do most anything to help their children get ahead, even go to ridiculous extremes to get special treatment from small things like doing their homework, to horrid things like killing a child's rival. The news is full of parents who go overboard for their children with the mistaken idea they are helping them out. Whoever thought to promote the Zebedee boys, whether parent or children, it is an all too common story of those who assume privilege for their offspring to the detriment of everyone in the community.

When I was growing up, it was hard for me to understand that sort of parental promotion and the motivation behind it. My brother was the only boy in the family, flanked by two sisters. It seemed to me, his younger sister, that my mother promoted him and watched out for him more than the rest of us. My child eyes saw the unfairness and bristled with anger whenever he got to do something special. We were close and fought a great deal because I felt I was as deserving as he was, yet I was often overlooked. When I grew up and became a parent, I found out several things from my mother that changed the way I viewed her, and the way she treated my brother.

My mother and I have the same blood type, A negative. When my first child was born and was A positive, I had to be given a drug to prevent a life-threatening blood interaction between me and my child, which also had to be done with my subsequent pregnancies. My mother had five children, but was pregnant eleven times. She lost the other babies to blood contamination, several long into the second and third trimesters. All of the babies were boys. When my brother was delivered, the cord was wrapped around his neck and he almost died. As a result, my mother was hardwired to protect and defend her little boy, even when he was no longer helpless or unable to help himself. She couldn't override the drive that was within her because of her recurring deep losses and constant fear. She knew her girls were all strong and scrappy and she didn't have to worry about us. Her sleeping and waking fears were about losing another son.

Chosen to Serve

Not the one who gets chosen first
but the puny, grubby one at line's end
the foolish ones who throw themselves
in any available leaf pile or snow bank
and who hold hands through life.

Not as a conqueror but as the meek
sweet, foolish lambs, wandering snacking
a green and yellow meadow lit by
light and sweet-grass flavored
with a willingness to love and forgive.

Not as CEOs but as janitors, not presidents
but front line enlisted, we offer our lives
from love that is greater than today's politics
an eternal love stronger than fraternity.

Not as leaders but as followers we take up
the cross of Jesus, we take up forgiveness
and reconciliation, a lightness of heart
and a child's willingness of hope and promise.

based on *Luke* 22:24–27

The roles of women and men, especially what was expected of young men and women growing up, are so different now than during biblical time that it is often hard for us to understand or unpack the stories that we read and hear. Basic rights that we assume to be universal cannot be assumed when we read scripture. It is sometimes difficult to find the intersection between our lives and the scriptures. The mystery and holiness of the Bible are found in the power of the stories to reach beyond the bounds of time and space, inviting us into relationship with God, pushing us beyond our own cultural and familial boundaries.

Girl Trouble: Martha and Mary

Now as they went on their way, he entered a certain village, where a woman named Martha welcomed him into her home. She had a sister named Mary, who sat at the Lord's feet and listened to what he was saying. But Martha was distracted by her many tasks; so she came to him and asked, "Lord, do you not care that my sister has left me to do all the work by myself? Tell her then to help me." But the Lord answered her, "Martha, Martha, you are worried and distracted by many things; there is need of only one thing. Mary has chosen the better part, which will not be taken away from her." (Luke 10:38–43)

The relationship between sisters is a most amazing construct, full of support and friendship. It can also be very challenging, both for the girls themselves and for their parents. As the mother of three girls, I can tell you that girls are both competitive and compassionate. They are loud and physical in different ways than boys, but in the same volume and consistency. They are very verbal at very young ages, and quickly learn how to work a room and how to face up to power, whether it is a teacher, a parent, or the ruler of the kingdom.

Luke's gospel offers the familiar story of Martha and Mary, the two women who were among those closest to Jesus. Their home was a second home for Jesus and they considered him family. There was always a place for him at their table; he never had to call ahead. He considered these women as close as sisters to him, although he had sisters of his own. His words to Martha must be taken from a place of familiarity, a place of family. They were words of love meant not to injure but to invite. Unfortunately for the Marthas of this world—and I include myself in the group—the story has been used to belittle our hard work and the importance of getting food on the table for the family and welcome guests. As a studious woman, one who has two masters' degrees and a doctorate, I have taken the time to sit at the Masters' feet. And yet, I have also stayed up deep into the night cleaning up after sick children and loading washing machines.

The story of Martha and Mary can be a dividing line among siblings. I am the third of the four sisters. My oldest and youngest sisters, Sherry and Betsy, are Marys. Pegi (who is now deceased) and I are the Marthas. Sherry, the oldest, was the best and most creative at squirreling out of chores. She had perfect timing when it came to washing dishes. She would have a bathroom emergency, bent over with cramps, pain, and nausea whenever it was her turn. We would have to take her place, temporarily of course, and she would find a way to stay in the bathroom until every dish was done and then, miraculously, her ailments vanished and she was able to return to the sink. Her timing was perfect; she was always saddened we had left nothing for her to do.

The "Mary" sisters, the bookends of this group of five siblings, had great dramatic skills even as small children and still apply them to this day. Nonetheless, both the Marthas and Marys of this world want to choose the better, more holy thing. I suggest, therefore, that Jesus was not chiding Martha, but inviting her to a role beyond where she had been placed by gender, tradition, circumstances, and family. Jesus was drawing her beyond the confines of her dictated jobs and the myriad of expectations upon her to a place of seeking deeper relationship with God, rather than the rag and mop. The invitation that Jesus extended to his beloved Martha was no less than earth shattering and headline making, thousands of years before the church ever took it seriously. Jesus wanted women walking beside him and following in his footsteps and in his ministry. Sad for all of us in the Christian Church worldwide that the leadership sided with the customs of the culture, rather than the call of God.

The relationship among sisters is complex, both undermined by society's expectations and buoyed by the close companionship of the shared spaces of bathrooms and kitchens. While my oldest sister was hiding from the dishes, my sister Pegi and I were learning to harmonize and dance together. She was seven years my elder but never distant. She always found ways to make tedium fun. We sang together and she taught me every pop and folk song she knew. We sang hymns and harmonized, making up funny lyrics when we needed to laugh out loud. I remember the music more than the chores and I know that I felt close to her in those many hours in the kitchen, our work becoming the medium for building relationship. It was a sudsy damp towel environment that encouraged harmony that required listening, blending, and a willingness to lean in towards another. Being part of a choir has been elemental to my life since I was a small child, and it was in these moments of chores and music that the choir became a part of me. I find God in singing with others. My sister Pegi and I, Marthas together, paved a road of knowing God in a deeper way, working side by side in the kitchen, finding out more about God's love in ways that sitting listening to the Rabbi could not reveal.

Martha and Mary are two sides of a personality design that all women know. Culture and tradition dictate specific roles, and those who chose another path find themselves defending themselves. Women are often expected to be innovative, traditional, and studious all at the same time. They are hardest on themselves and on one another, judging by standards they do not want to be judged by. Jesus loved these two women, understanding the depth and complexity of their relationship, and invited them to sit and enjoy the love that God had for them. How revolutionary! A man inviting a woman to sit as a disciple, as a student at the Rabbi's feet, an equal in a very unequal world. The story of Martha and Mary is not an invitation to division but rather an invitation to sing in the choir, to harmonize with all the people, and to be a unique voice blended in the mix of a rich and vibrant witness.

The first time I attended a clergy meeting, as an ordained person in 1989, we were gathered for the opening Eucharist in the Cathedral of the Incarnation in Baltimore, Maryland. It was a beautiful fall day and the turnout was excellent. In those days, there were only a few women among a sea of men. When we joined in the first hymn, I was blown away and then moved to tears. It was a rich tenor, bass, and baritone harmony, a reverberating choir, almost devoid of all the higher melodic registers. My voice was lost in the thunderous sound, as were the voices of the few other women in the cathedral. I was grateful in that moment to be welcomed into a community and colleague group that was so recently shuttered to women, and also saddened for the loss over so many generations, saddened for the insight of Marthas and Marys everywhere, who had so much to offer, so much music and harmony to add to the rich inheritance of the followers of Christ.

Years later, when I became a bishop, I attended my first House of Bishops meeting in Texas. Again, the voices were almost completely male and I was reminded how beautiful the whole range of voices is, and how empty I felt without them all. When I was a little girl, I saw a movie about the Vienna Boys' Choir and had dreamed of being a part of it. My voice would never change, I imagined, and I could be part of that wonderful musical tradition and sing all over the world. When I got home from Texas, I realized I had fulfilled my childhood dream in a very real way. I was part of the boys' choir and we would sing together in many places of the world. Unfortunately, there are still very few women among the throng of choristers, and many places in our communion still forbid women to participate in the life and leadership of the church. Harmony and cooperation are not often sought over power and control, even within the Christian Church.

In this chapter we have focused on the relationships that develop as we develop, the growing children among other children, and the task of finding our place in family and society as we develop a personal and individual sense of spirituality and relationship with God. In my family, we grew into the hand-me-downs we were given. When one of us had the opportunity to pick out something for herself, or even better, to purchase something new, we found a deeper sense of individuality and personal integrity. Who we were had become something more than our small family identity, and yet we were still entwined in the fabric of family, faith, and community.

Though for the most part we survive our growing up years, we move into adulthood with the gifts and scars that we develop during our formative years. Domestic violence, abuse, and substance problems are all too common in families, and in some societies still openly condoned at some level. Children are exposed to a myriad of psychological and emotional damage while they are tender and growing, and these exposures can often cripple one's capacity to develop a positive self-image and contribute to a warped sense of God. Growing up strong in personality, conviction, and faith is difficult to accomplish for anyone, even under the best of circumstances. In the coming chapters we will talk more about the ways we can engage the scripture stories as we rewrite our future of faith.

CHAPTER 2 * REFLECTION

Exercises and Questions

Hopefully you have begun a journal and are finding places of connection (and some disconnect) with the scriptures. You are in the process of weaving your story into the biblical stories, finding God revealed in your own life as you see yourself in the larger narrative.

A simple group exercise might be to bring pictures of your family and siblings, and share a few stories of growing up in your family. It might be helpful to describe your faith traditions as a child growing up, and what you were told about God and your relationship to the divine.

1. What kind of foods were important in your family and why?

2. How did the adults in your life deal with conflict?

3. What were the expected roles in your family? Were there different roles based on birth order, gender, skills, or other priorities?

4. Who taught you the most about God? How did they do that?

⇜ CHAPTER 3 ⇝

Inheritance and Tradition: Eating with Pigs Again

This chapter will focus on the relationships among adult children in extended families. No matter what we face in our families, maturing and taking responsibility for ourselves is a learning process and a struggle. Our relationships as adult siblings can help us build a sustainable life or they can continue and magnify the ongoing roles and feuds that began in childhood. As adults, our relationship with God is primarily our responsibility; what came before in our families can help us desire to grow into that responsibility or to drive us to reject any walk in faith we might have inherited. As I wrote in the introduction, genuine authentic faith is identified with the ongoing process of forgiveness, redemption, and creativity. Seeing others with God's eyes means seeing creative capacity where we never expected it. Seeing ourselves in the eyes of God, with the creative capacity to participate with God in the redemption of the world, is even more difficult. We grow into our faith and theology not by isolating ourselves from others, but from expanding their creative capacity and ours. In many biblical stories we find siblings participating in the return and redemption of their families, struggling inside and out with that explosive mixture of love and fury that is generated between family members. Those closest to us can irritate us very quickly. They know our buttons well and they like to push them. Yet, it is this yeasty place that scripture seems to find most holy, the incubator of irrational anger and fear as well as the deepest love. God finds us in our weakness with all of our soft spots and remakes and renews us right from there, not the other way around.

When I was a little girl I wanted to be a minister like my daddy. I was probably six or seven when I had some sense of call. Of course it was a child's idea, probably from some dream one night. I told my friend, who laughed at me and reminded me I was a girl. I told my grandmother who was staying with us about it and she told me that only my brother could be a minister, as only men were called. Slowly but surely a role that I truly desired was put aside and scratched off my hopes and dreams list. I was a tomboy, that was certain, and many of my ideas were thought absurd for a girl to have. I was laughed at and taunted and told that I was just trying to be like my brother.

We all receive messages in all sorts of ways from family and culture that say no to our creativity, no to our imagination, no the possibilities we dream. By the time we reach adulthood, many of us have sought the safe harbor of appropriate roles and jobs. Yet God doesn't give up on us even when the world gives up on us or when we give up on ourselves. The One who created us uniquely and wondrously also aches for us to be completely ourselves, to overflow with confidence in the awesomeness of our creation. Very few people truly find that deep self-acceptance—that integration of body, mind, and spirit that we were all created to discover. We spend so much time hiding and repackaging ourselves to match the models we have been given that we get lost in our own self-translation.

After I was all grown up and the mother of two little girls, I could no longer suppress my sense of call. I tried every way possible to wriggle out of it and translate it into something acceptable and understandable to my family and society. My husband, who had encouraged me all along the way, was willing to support me in the endeavor. I was reluctant and sure that I would meet with failure. I heard all the voices down all the years who told me it was a role in which I did not belong. I finally came up with a plan. I could fulfill God's call and continue working with children and young people if I studied for a master's degree in Christian education. I thought it was the perfect solution: an honorable role long held by influential women, and it fulfilled my call to serve.

I was feeling quite intelligent and clever with my plan when I finally called my dad. I told him I had a call to ministry and that I was going to apply to Princeton Seminary for a degree in Christian Education. My father was quiet for a moment, and then said, "Carol, if God is calling you to the ministry, don't you think you need to be faithful and follow that call? A degree is Christian Ed. is okay but (he hesitated) no one is going to respect you. If God is calling you have to be faithful."

I felt hot tears roll down my face and I knew he was right in everything. I thought he would laugh at me. I thought he could never imagine his daughter in this way. Yet he was telling me to stop avoiding God and follow where my Creator was leading me. I felt free and terrified all at the same time.

It is important to share that my dad had been a military chaplain and was very conservative. He wasn't against less than traditional roles for his daughters, but he struggled to live into changing roles as the world changed in front of and around him. He wanted a family that was traditional and faithful more than anything. I think my call to ordination in another denomination in a very different time frightened him, although he never admitted it to me. When I was ordained a deacon, he was proudly there; when I was ordained a priest, he wore his robes and laid his hands on me with all the other Episcopal clergy gathered there. He didn't live to see me elected or consecrated a bishop, nor did he see me graduated from Princeton with a master's in Christian education, nor when I was awarded my Ph.D. But he was there. His love and spirit that drove him to see the possibilities in me even when he didn't really understand it, are gifts that continue to redeem and encourage me every day.

Dad

I thought I buried you
I know the funeral was proper and complete.
Black clad mourners,
sad long faces
deep low organ music
the smell of lilies signaling death.

I thought I buried you and yet you're here
you are in my dreams
behind my eyes
torturing me to behold the world
as you would.

Did you die to set me free to love you
or did you keep your distance in life
so we can now be one?

My hands and freckles are yours
and the depth and roundness
your voice spoken
breath for breath in mine.

You are my dream life visitor
and my bodily guest
aching me to know you
as a friend.

Erik Erikson describes adolescence as the stage of fidelity, when we are struggling with our own identity is contrast with the roles we have been given. It is a time of questioning when we ask ourselves where we fit in and where we are going in life, when we take the roles we have been given and tear them apart to remake them for ourselves. It can be a very painful period of life and it can be elongated by many modern challenges. Erikson believed that the role of parents in this stage of development was to encourage exploration and to support their children's choices for their own identity. He found that under the hand of stricter, more controlling parents who push their offspring to conformity, an adolescent will suffer from much identity confusion and some-times live a life of hidden or even multiple identities. Society and families can make the job of growing up a complicated produc-tion, often hindering development and exploration rather than encouraging it.

Likewise, our spiritual growth can be caught in the stranglehold of identity and role confusion. If we were taken to church as a child, we might have celebrated some rite of passage, such as Confirmation, and then found there was no place for us in the life of that same church which claimed we were now adult members. The worship, education, and outreach activities of many religious organizations separate the teens into a small group and then plan nothing for them when they become young adults. Many families who insisted on religious participation for their younger child, move their focus to college and career and away from faith. Academics and sports take primacy in the ordered life of their young person. In the time when young people need play, exploration, and experimentation, the responsible adults are pushing for more structure, more decisions, and more clarity, leaving the young people with little clarity and massive curiosity. As teens and young adults we ache to understand who we are, where we are going, and who is going with us. We ache to know the depths of our souls. We seek expressions that help us define these for ourselves. Music and other expressive arts place an incredible role in the search for a meaningful and authentic identity.

Our Cherokee traditions are focused in rituals that cleanse and renew both individuals and relationships. Part of growing up among my people is the expectation that we take on more personal respon-sibility for healing and forgiveness, for making amends, and bearing the pain of broken relationships as we grow. The Green Corn Ceremony was traditionally celebrated during late June or early July for about four days. The dates scheduled for the celebration depended on when the first corn ripened. The ceremony was held in the middle of the ceremonial grounds. Included in the rituals were the stomp dance, the feather dance, and the buffalo dances. At certain points of the ceremonies the people fasted, played stickball, sacrificed corn, and took medicine. After the ceremonial fasting they would feast. Another ritual was rinsing themselves in water and having prayer. They believed a cleansing washes away impurities or bad deeds and started a new life. The cleansing ceremony was performed by a priest and was followed with fasting and praying.

Running on Empty: Jacob and Esau

As soon as Isaac had finished blessing Jacob, when Jacob had scarcely gone out from the presence of his father Isaac, his brother Esau came in from his hunting. He also prepared savory food, and brought it to his father. And he said to his father, "Let my father sit up and eat of his son's game, so that you may bless me." His father Isaac said to him, "Who are you?" He answered, "I am your firstborn son, Esau." Then Isaac trembled violently, and said, "Who was it then that hunted game and brought it to me, and I ate it all before you came, and I have blessed him?—yes, and blessed he shall be!" When Esau heard his father's words, he cried out with an exceedingly great and bitter cry, and said to his father, "Bless me, me also, father!" But he said, "Your brother came deceitfully, and he has taken away your blessing." Esau said, "Is he not rightly named Jacob? For he has supplanted me these two times. He took away my birthright; and look, now he has taken away my blessing." Then he said, "Have you not reserved a blessing for me?" Isaac answered Esau, "I have already made him your lord, and I have given him all his brothers as servants, and with grain and wine I have sustained him. What then can I do for you, my son?" Esau said to his father, "Have you only one blessing, father? Bless me, me also, father!" And Esau lifted up his voice and wept. Then his father Isaac answered him: "See, away from the fatness of the earth shall your home be, and away from the dew of heaven on high. By your sword you shall live and you shall serve your brother; but when you break loose, you shall break his yoke from your neck."

Now Esau hated Jacob because of the blessing with which his father had blessed him, and Esau said to himself, "The days of mourning for my father are approaching; then I will kill my brother Jacob." But the words of her elder son Esau were told to Rebekah; so she sent and called her younger son Jacob and said to him, "Your brother Esau is consoling himself by planning to kill you. Now therefore, my son, obey my voice; flee at once to my brother Laban in Haran, and stay with him for a while, until your brother's fury turns away—until your brother's anger against you turns away, and he forgets what you have done to him; then I will send, and bring you back from there. Why should I lose both of you in one day?" (Genesis 27:30–45)

The capacity of siblings, especially those on the cusp of adulthood, to anger and betray one another seems like a given in families. As we find our way from our initial identity struggles to our first loves, we are often at odds with the other children who share our bloodline. We can't imagine how we could be from the same family. We can find our siblings abhorrent and embarrassing, as if the earlier embarrassment that was triggered by our parents, now is cast as a mantle onto our siblings. It may be that we are too alike, or that they know our weaknesses and our vulnerabilities, but somehow adult or near adult siblings can drive each other crazy. In the extremes, as with Jacob and Esau, murder is contemplated and Dad's advice is to get gone. Isaac's admonition seems rooted in his own self-protection as much as in his concern for his child. He was the cause of the dissention in the first place, giving only one blessing and one inheritance. He had twins, a gift from God, which now he seems to want to fling apart instead of finding a way to bring them together. He would have to buck tradition and laws to do so, and he seems unable to step outside of the cultural restraints in order to heal the rift he has caused.

And yet God, in his mighty love, might challenge us to think deeper into this story. The boys are becoming men, and as individuals, they are growing apart for many reasons. They are very different, differently gifted and differently-abled. Jacob might have stayed with his mother forever, if he didn't have to run for his life. And Esau might have fought (and lost) Jacob for women, if he even allowed Jacob to live after such a heinous betrayal.

When I left for college in 1973, I was not embarking on the usual dorm and parent drop-off experience. I was going to be a poet and musician and I had chosen to attend Antioch College at one of their satellite centers in Baltimore. This meant I was on my own to find a room to rent and there were not the usual safety arrangements that comfort parents at least a little. I would have to bus all over the city. After I registered, my dad and mom helped me find a room to rent with another student the office had recommended. It was all very iffy and at seventeen I thought it was great pondering that I would be an adult and free of them in a few quick moments. I wanted more than anything to be away from my little sister who was just starting middle school and my older brother who was still living at home while going to college. I wanted the whole scene behind me.

Later that afternoon they stopped to visit at an old friend's house. These people were old seminary friends of my dad's and they fed us a wonderful dinner. My parents had to leave that evening, so I was to stay the night with my hosts. They promised to get me to where I was going in the morning, which they did. When my parents' car pulled out of the driveway, the cool that I had known for all that time in preparation and planning, in getting a room and saying goodbye, melted away. I was a weeping pile of goo. The nice minister's wife held me as I cried and said very little. They had lived for a long time in East Baltimore and had seen their community slide from middle class to deep poverty. She was tender with me but also realistic. This is what I chose to do, and I could call my folks and go home or stick it out and move one. She wrote her phone number on a card and offered any help I needed, but reminded me that I was the one making choices, and I was the one who had to deal with the consequences. She brought me up short in those few moments and helped me to grow up tremendously. She said things that my parents couldn't say, and in ways that I could hear.

Looking back, I have to marvel at my parents' strength and love to let me go. Baltimore was not the safest city in the early 1970s and I was still just a kid at seventeen despite my belief to the contrary. But they let me go and prayed hard, and knew that I was going to have to grow up and make choices. They could no longer protect me and they had done their best and now it was time to let go. With three older siblings, two of whom were married by then, they had a bit of practice letting go. It is not easy for a parent or the child. Both have to separate and reach for others, no matter how scary and ambivalent the partings and moving on might be.

The Parable of the Prodigal and His Brother

Then Jesus said, "There was a man who had two sons. The younger of them said to his father, 'Father, give me the share of the property that will belong to me.' So he divided his property between them. A few days later the younger son gathered all he had and travelled to a distant country, and there he squandered his property in dissolute living. When he had spent everything, a severe famine took place throughout that country, and he began to be in need. So he went and hired himself out to one of the citizens of that country, who sent him to his fields to feed the pigs. He would gladly have filled himself with the pods that the pigs were eating; and no one gave him anything. But when he came to himself he said, 'How many of my father's hired hands have bread enough and to spare, but here I am dying of hunger! I will get up and go to my father, and I will say to him, "Father, I have sinned against heaven and before you; I am no longer worthy to be called your son; treat me like one of your hired hands.'" So he set off and went to his father. But while he was still far off, his father saw him and was filled with compassion; he ran and put his arms around him and kissed him. Then the son said to him, 'Father, I have sinned against heaven and before you; I am no longer worthy to be called your son.' But the father said to his slaves, 'Quickly, bring out a robe—the best one—and put it on him; put a ring on his finger and sandals on his feet. And get the fatted calf and kill it, and let us eat and celebrate; for this son of mine was dead and is alive again; he was lost and is found!' And they began to celebrate.

"Now his elder son was in the field; and when he came and approached the house, he heard music and dancing. He called one of the slaves and asked what was going on. He replied, 'Your brother has come, and your father has killed the fatted calf, because he has got him back safe and sound.' Then he became angry and refused to go in. His father came out and began to plead with him. But he answered his father, 'Listen! For all these years I have been working like a slave for you, and I have never disobeyed your command; yet you have never given me even a young goat so that I might celebrate with my friends. But when this son of yours came back, who has devoured your property with prostitutes, you killed the fatted calf for him!' Then the father said to him, 'Son, you are always with me, and all that is mine is yours.'" (Luke 15:11–31)

This terribly familiar story of the prodigal is so deeply embedded in our culture and history as a nation and as Christians that many have a very hard time unpacking the story and gaining new insight into it. We find a rebellious and angry young man who goes off on his own and flounders. Returning and begging forgiveness, he gets the best of everything and ticks off his older brother royally. The young prodigal becomes the restless cowboy, the archetype of the American male with all the swagger and bravado movies can muster. Since movies are the modern American narrative, the stories that bind our culture together, then the prodigal is often the most worshipped hero in our modern day. Simply look at football players, movie idols, and other celebrities who have fallen from grace only to rise higher in everyone's esteem after some tearful admission and the socially acceptable, often legally required time spent in rehab. The coolest people go to rehab these days and we idolize them for their bravery as well as their physical prowess and acting skills. Meanwhile, all the right living, faithful other children, whether older or younger in the family, never get a party, the fatted calf (a blowout at the country club in modern parlance), or any regard for their constancy.

When looking at this story, folks often overlook the set up and the final lines. Jesus begins this story by saying that the kingdom of heaven is like this, and ends by saying, "child, you are always with me, and all that is mine is yours." The story is about the forgiveness that is available to all, as is the rejoicing when we turn back from the terrible mistakes we make. But the story is much more than simply understanding rewards can be had when confessing and making amends. Many couples fight just so they can "kiss and make up." Seeking love's reward by hurting and lashing out is a very dysfunctional way of living within relationships, but it is all too common in life. Jesus could have ignored the older brother and left him out of the story. Instead, he does what all good storytellers do, adding depth and color—he ends with a moral, or in this case a promise: all is yours and you are always with me, embedded in my heart. The prodigals may get the limelight and the flash in the pan, but you get it all, now and always. You are a part of me, inseparable, bound heart and soul to the God of love.

So many people are prodigals and so many are older brothers, and most of us are a crazy, inconsistent mix of both. God speaks to us in our anxiety of belonging and says to both and more, welcome back, you are always with me, part of me, belonging in the heart of God. When we focus only on the prodigal, we go for the glamour, and when we focus on the older son, we can pit one child against the other. When we welcome all parts of our nature into the story and see the totality of the narrative, we understand that no one is left outside of the circle.

Many years ago, a call came that is hard to receive in any family at any time. A sibling was taken to rehab, having been found in what can only be described as dangerous and troubling circumstances. It was rehab or jail. I was called on to drive my mother to this place, more than five hours away, and the trip was made all the more anxious as a terrible rainstorm set in. We were heading out of town and the rain began. Since it was summer, people poured off the beaches in droves. The water pummeled us as we sat in traffic, inching along, and as the minutes wore by and the anxiety and tension built up, silence gave way to tears and tears, finally, to laughter. The five-hour trip took more like eight hours. Somehow in our terrified state, God supplied us with humor. We had a sense of not having anything to fear despite the overwhelming challenges that we knew lay ahead. When we arrived at the motel we had arranged for in the middle of the night, we found out it was frequented by ladies of the evening; it was too late to turn around and find another room. We secured our doors and prayed for our safety in this sketchy neighborhood, knowing somehow we were going to be all right. We couldn't help but laugh at our situation. We were acting in love, reaching out to one in danger of being lost, and whatever we had before us, we were embedded in the heart of God. Somehow we found laughter through it all, and so many years later, God's love healed the most broken and the most prodigal among us.

An Older Child's Lament

Standing at a distance
fists knotted stiff by my side
the house exploding joy
doors slamming everyone rushing
I wish to walk away
from this celebration.

Jealous, green deep and rolling
a tidal wave in my belly
rolling over and over tears
sting hot and dry to bitter
salt on my face.

Blood like my blood, ruddy complexion
like mine too, a strong body thinned
by depravity and disease running
weeping to my father's arms.

The arms that won't even reach out
pat me on the back, nor lend a hand
when down and covered in the sweat dirt
of his rich fields and my duty
I am never drawn to his chest as
he holds him now.

I want to know love like the lost
the belligerent the toddler
turned terrorist turning our family upside
down aching for the lost broken child.

Oh father, I too am broken and lost
I am sinking to my knees in my own sorrow
it lies like a blanket wet and warm over me
night and day I cry for the embrace
the assurance of love.

based on *Luke* 15:17–32

You Have to Hide Your Love Away

When Jacob learned that there was grain in Egypt, he said to his sons, "Why do you keep looking at one another? I have heard," he said, "that there is grain in Egypt; go down and buy grain for us there, that we may live and not die." So ten of Joseph's brothers went down to buy grain in Egypt. But Jacob did not send Joseph's brother Benjamin with his brothers, for he feared that harm might come to him. Thus the sons of Israel were among the other people who came to buy grain, for the famine had reached the land of Canaan.

Now Joseph was governor over the land; it was he who sold to all the people of the land. And Joseph's brothers came and bowed themselves before him with their faces to the ground. When Joseph saw his brothers, he recognized them, but he treated them like strangers and spoke harshly to them. "Where do you come from?" he said. They said, "From the land of Canaan, to buy food." Although Joseph had recognized his brothers, they did not recognize him. Joseph also remembered the dreams that he had dreamed about them. He said to them, "You are spies; you have come to see the nakedness of the land!" They said to him, "No, my lord; your servants have come to buy food. We are all sons of one man; we are honest men; your servants have never been spies." But he said to them, "No, you have come to see the nakedness of the land!" They said, "We, your servants, are twelve brothers, the sons of a certain man in the land of Canaan; the youngest, however, is now with our father, and one is no more." But Joseph said to them, "It is just as I have said to you; you are spies! Here is how you shall be tested: as Pharaoh lives, you shall not leave this place unless your youngest brother comes here! Let one of you go and bring your brother, while the rest of you remain in prison, in order that your words may be tested, whether there is truth in you; or else, as Pharaoh lives, surely you are spies." And he put them all together in prison for three days.

On the third day Joseph said to them, "Do this and you will live, for I fear God: if you are honest men, let one of your brothers stay here where you are imprisoned. The rest of you shall go and carry grain for the famine of your households, and bring your youngest brother to me. Thus your words will be verified, and you shall not die." And they agreed to do so. They said to one another, "Alas, we are paying the penalty for what we did to our brother; we saw his anguish when he pleaded with us, but we would not listen. That is why this anguish has come upon us." Then Reuben answered them, "Did I not tell you not to wrong the boy? But you would not listen. So now there comes a reckoning for his blood." They did not know that Joseph understood them, since he spoke with them through an interpreter. He turned away from them and wept; then he returned and spoke to them. And he picked out Simeon and had him bound before their eyes. Joseph then gave orders to fill their bags with grain, to return every man's money to his sack, and to give them provisions for their journey. This was done for them.

They loaded their donkeys with their grain, and departed. When one of them opened his sack to give his donkey fodder at the lodging-place, he saw his money at the top of the sack. He said to his brothers, "My money has been put back; here it is in my sack!" At this they lost heart and turned trembling to one another, saying, "What is this that God has done to us?"

When they came to their father Jacob in the land of Canaan, they told him all that had happened to them, saying, "The man, the lord of the land, spoke harshly to us, and charged us with spying on the land. But we said to him, 'We are honest men, we are not spies. We are twelve brothers, sons of our father; one is no more, and the youngest is now with our father in the land of Canaan.' Then the man, the lord of the land, said to us, 'By this I shall know that you are honest men: leave one of your brothers with me, take grain for the famine of your households, and go your way. Bring your youngest brother to me, and I shall know that you are not spies but honest men. Then I will release your brother to you, and you may trade in the land.' "

As they were emptying their sacks, there in each one's sack was his bag of money. When they and their father saw their bundles of money, they were dismayed. And their father Jacob said to them, "I am the one you have bereaved of children: Joseph is no more, and Simeon is no more, and now you would take Benjamin. All this has happened to me!" Then Reuben said to his father, "You may kill my two sons if I do not bring him back to you. Put him in my hands, and I will bring him back to you." But he said, "My son shall not go down with you, for his brother is dead, and he alone is left. If harm should come to him on the journey that you are to make, you would bring down my grey hairs with sorrow to Sheol." (Genesis 42)

I include this story of Joseph and his brothers in later life, not just because I love the story itself, but also because is a foreshadowing of the reconciliation that is to come. It is the set up for the final chapters of rekindled affection and renewed relationship that can and does happen with siblings who are estranged. I am captivated by the scene, as if it is something right out of Shakespeare's *Twelfth Night*: some people disguising themselves and pretending to not recognize one another, while others are completely fooled but sense grave danger. Siblings are pitted against one another and the adults and community around them for survival's sake. It makes for extraordinary drama, yet most of our sibling rivalries and estrangements are less mythical in size and scope. This story of Joseph at his zenith, when he uses his gifts and powers ultimately for good, is more than an engaging piece of theater. The ensuing drama and reconciliation help us examine our own personal challenges with new insights.

It hurts as an adult to be left out of family things. When our chosen profession or choice of partners is shunned or disregarded by our parents and siblings, we can find ourselves terribly hurt and reactive. Imagine Joseph, who longed for a family, whose brothers left him for dead, and whose only crime was being favored by his father. His father's favoritism and affection had infected and soured a whole family. Estrangement built on estrangement and hostility was the *lingua franca*. Then crisis and need broke in, which are often God's chosen tools for reuniting families and leading people to find forgiveness and renewal. We usually need to be forced to acknowledge our need before we can open ourselves to one another. A Presbyterian friend of my dad used to say, "Embarrassment is first step of healing. When we acknowledge our need and our humanity, God can work with us and among for the change we pine for."

Often among adult siblings, distance and time can erect such barriers that we never get the chance to scale them and find healing. Finding no resolution during one's lifetime is a sad end to the story. It happened in my family. My grandfather passed away one early December and it was a difficult time for us all. Several of my mother's siblings who had not reconciled with their father for a host of reasons did not attend the funeral. My mother was strong in the midst of it, but it was evident to me as a young teenager that it was painful and strenuous for her. She ached to have her broken family mended and at peace. The pain of alcoholism, poverty, abuse, and displacement had scarred them all.

We were at home trimming our tree a few days before Christmas; we were never ones to be ahead of the season. We liked to linger with the season, to prepare late into the night on Christmas Eve and then collapse in a pile, exhausted for the next few days. The life of a clergy family is unique and complicated during holiday seasons. The phone rang and my father answered and had a brief professional conversation with an old colleague. He asked us to excuse ourselves for a minute and then invited us to come back in. My mother was crying. He explained that a pastor he knew from Rhode Island had just buried a man in a potter's field. It was a cold and snowy day, I recall, and as we huddled around my mother, she seemed peaceful despite her tears. My father went on to say that the man had been identified as Bruce WalkingStick and the pastor knew that was my mother's name. He thought some family should know. Bruce, my grandfather's kid brother who had been lost to alcohol, poverty, and wandering, was now at rest. At the end of his troubled, tortured life he had been buried with dignity and compassion because some good person had gone out of their way to care for a stranger. Our flesh and blood are too often only united in death.

In this third chapter we have looked at the relationships of siblings, and how these relationships form our growing both physically and spiritually. We grow up side by side in families, and yet we find ourselves often very different. God speaks to us in the midst of these relationships, encouraging us to creatively find ourselves and our faith in the midst of this complex and often terrifying community. Whether we are a family because of similar DNA or by design and choice, we grow in faith and love by testing one another's limits. What we often find in our siblings is a reflection of God: a love that is willing to stretch beyond the limits, beyond our brokenness and anger, and beyond all reasonable hope to bring us back home.

Prayer

When I whisper in the night
sleepless anxious turning troubled
a world of tomorrows churning
my brain alight with inevitable dangers
you hear my breaking voice and whisper
back in song.

When I shout in agony loss
like a deep flooding river swirling
carrying me down stream to grief city
a dark and fathomless ache
is answered by your warm arms.

When I laugh joy bubbling
a child face dirty and thrilled
small accomplishments beaming
knees and elbows missing teeth
life is full and you are
sunlight and gold May afternoons.

When silent overcome and shivering
in a winter room with frost around
windows bleak with early sunset
rooms shadowed and dusty with remorse
you are a little bell shimmering
sound in the silent twilight.

And when I lay down in final rest
amidst ancestors and enemies friends
all deeds complete all prayers accomplished
you will breath with me in the light
and walk within us prayer as breathing
prayer as light.

CHAPTER 3 • REFLECTION

Exercises and Questions

This is a good time to break into small groups of two or three to discuss the following questions:

1. Who encouraged you to find your identity as you were growing up?

2. Who or what held you back, and what divisions kept you from knowing your siblings and family better?

3. What music, media, culture, and/or customs resonated with you as you explored your unique identity?

4. Are there ways you are still grasping with identity?

5. What scriptures in this chapter helped you know yourself better?

6. Who might you reach out to for further reflection on identity?

7. At this session, folks might want to share cultural experiences that were defining for them.

This may be a good time to write a prayer for yourselves, both as an individual and as a group. The group may want to identify specific needs that the discussions have raised up. This prayer can be used as a gathering prayer at each subsequent meeting.

Individuals in the group might want to take the group prayer and refine it personally for their daily use at home. The importance of a regular prayer that can be recited in many times and places cannot be emphasized enough. The group prayer can be put on a small piece of paper and tucked in a pocket so that it is readily available in times of stress and anxiety. It reminds us all that we are not alone.

Marriage and Fidelity: Finding Love in all the Wrong Places

As we move forward, we find ourselves in the complicated world of adult relationships and expectations. We have moved beyond the struggle for initial personality integration and identity to that place where we want to share our lives with one another. Erikson calls this stage of young adulthood simply Love: the time when we focus on intimacy in our family and work relationships. Our anxieties center around questions dealing with the contrast between intimacy and isolation. Erikson suggests this period lasts from the mid-twenties through our early forties. The common questions concern our partners and our long-term goals, the loss of identity when in relationship, and the conflict between work and identity within the relationship. In our present times, this stage has become elongated as societies permit young men and women to explore longer and do not require settling by a certain age, as might have been in the past.

Depending on our families of origin, our race, our culture, and our financial status, this period can be both extremely hazardous and complicated; it can also be relatively short. Women in many places around the world are expected to be wives and mothers before their twentieth year; the decisions as to the who and how they marry are prescribed for them. In the United States, we outwardly say that young people are expected to study and explore into their late twenties, and there are no rules for when folks should settle down with a partner. We are really a people of many cultures and sub-cultures within those, such that there is no clear age bracket in my mind to define this time of "love" as Erikson so amorphously puts it. For many young people, this is the time when we show others who we have found ourselves to be, hoping for someone who will love us in our completeness. More often than not, this is an awkward and painful time in people's lives, as standards of beauty and physical prowess often leave many marginalized. The powerful influence of the media, the internet, and the daily bombardment of advertising add to the complexities and pressures felt by those in this stage of life.

I was at the end of my first year in college when I met my husband. I was eighteen and ready for a summer working on the beach and hanging out with old friends. It was then, right before I left Baltimore for the summer, that I met Mark. I had told a dear friend that I was looking forward to making no attachments that summer, since relationships and the ensuing mess only got in the way of enjoying oneself. I had the most wonderful plans for a season of independence, music, and poetry and was looking forward to spending my days on the beach and my nights playing guitar, writing songs, and reveling in the safety and companionship of old friends. I met Mark just a few days before leaving town, and I knew I was smitten. I also knew God's hand was in it. Why? Because, in my experience, when you say your plans out loud, especially when one is as smug and self-righteous as I was at eighteen, God finds a way to turn things in a new direction and invite us into extraordinary places that our small minds could never imagine. God invites us to let go of control so that we can experience extraordinary blessings.

Less than a year later, after an eleven-month courtship, Mark and I married. I was nineteen and he was twenty-three. None of our friends was getting married. This was the mid-seventies; marriage, especially among the artsy crowd we hung with, was something people's parents did—an old-fashioned way of life. We knew early on we wanted to get married and were young enough to ignore the wisdom of the day. We were married in a joint Catholic and Protestant service, with my father and a priest presiding. We were married on a Thursday in May and had our reception on the lawn outside the church. The ceremony was simple, plenty enough for us, and the marriage has lasted more than thirty-six years. What began as a change in plans, a detour from my expectations, has become a way of life, the ground of my being, and a relationship that has changed everything for the better. Most often, we plan and God laughs, because it seems that God's ideas are bigger than ours, God's creativity is more limitless, and God's possibilities often don't figure in our thinking at all.

Detours

Too often gapers delay the route we
turn and see the broken wreak humanity
splayed across our paths and time stands
still traffic stalls and we grope and
creep to find another way home.

The exit in sight we turn to strangers
who offer another way and we follow
through gardened suburban lanes lined
busy streets and foreign territory
we never planned to see.

We are changed by what we see relieved
to be home again clinging
to the wonder of love and familiar.

God is the Creator of detours those paths
where we learn to trust and be lost
to the moment and the other.

We are known and loved in our detours
we are made whole in our brokenness
by the Lamb of God who tarried with strangers
and called sinners his companions
and tattered women as disciples.

The scripture stories that follow can help us articulate the challenges and blessings of living in the midst of new relationships and the chaos that swirls around us as we explore another and ourselves anew in relationship. First, I want to describe a wedding and marriage tradition that is very different from our present-day concept of an American wedding. The Cherokee wedding ceremony is a very beautiful event, whether it is the old fashioned or 'ancient' ceremony or a modern one. The original ceremony differed from clan to clan and community to community, but used the same basic elements. Because clanship is matrilineal in the Cherokee society, one is forbidden to marry within one's own clan. Because the woman holds the family clan, she is represented at the ceremony by both her mother (and clan mother) and oldest brother. The brother stands with her as his vow to take the responsibility of teaching the children in spiritual and religious matters, as that is the traditional role of the uncle (*e-du-tsi*). In ancient times, they would meet at the center of the townhouse. The groom was accompanied by his mother.

After the sacred spot for the ceremony has been blessed for seven consecutive days, it was time for the ceremony. The bride and groom approached the sacred fire and were blessed by the priest or priestess. All participants in the wedding, including guests, were also blessed. Songs were sung in Cherokee, and those conducting the ceremony blessed the couple. Both the bride and groom were covered in a blue blanket. At the right point of the ceremony, the priest or priestess removed each blue blanket, and covered the couple together with one white blanket, indicating the beginning of their new life together.

Instead of exchanging rings, in the old times the couple exchanged food. The groom brought ham or venison, or some other meat, to indicate his intention to provide for the household. The bride provided corn or beanbread to symbolize her willingness to care for and provide nourishment for her household. On a side note, when a baby is born, the traditional question is, "Is it a bow, or a sifter?" Even at birth, the male is associated with hunting and providing, and the female with nourishing and giving life. The gifts of meat and corn also honor the fact that traditionally, Cherokee men hunted for the household, while women tended the farms. It also reflects the roles of *Kanati* (first man) and *Selu* (first woman).

The couple drank together from a Cherokee Wedding Vase. The vessel held one drink, but had two openings for the couple to drink from at the same time. Following the ceremony, the town, community, or clans provided a wedding feast, and the dancing and celebrating often continued all night. Today, some Cherokee traditionalists still observe portions of these wedding rituals. The vows of today's ceremony reflect the Cherokee culture and belief system, but are in other ways similar to wedding ceremonies of other cultures.

Did You Ever Have to Make Up Your Mind? Two Daughters, Too Many Choices

Then Laban said to Jacob, "Because you are my kinsman, should you therefore serve me for nothing? Tell me, what shall your wages be?" Now Laban had two daughters; the name of the elder was Leah, and the name of the younger was Rachel. Leah's eyes were lovely, and Rachel was graceful and beautiful. Jacob loved Rachel; so he said, "I will serve you seven years for your younger daughter Rachel." Laban said, "It is better that I give her to you than that I should give her to any other man; stay with me." So Jacob served seven years for Rachel, and they seemed to him but a few days because of the love he had for her.

Then Jacob said to Laban, "Give me my wife that I may go in to her, for my time is completed." So Laban gathered together all the people of the place, and made a feast. But in the evening he took his daughter Leah and brought her to Jacob; and he went in to her. (Laban gave his maid Zilpah to his daughter Leah to be her maid.) When morning came, it was Leah! And Jacob said to Laban, "What is this you have done to me? Did I not serve with you for Rachel? Why then have you deceived me?" Laban said, "This is not done in our country—giving the younger before the firstborn. Complete the week of this one, and we will give you the other also in return for serving me for another seven years." Jacob did so, and completed her week; then Laban gave him his daughter Rachel as a wife. (Laban gave his maid Bilhah to his daughter Rachel to be her maid.) So Jacob went in to Rachel also, and he loved Rachel more than Leah. He served Laban for another seven years.

When the Lord saw that Leah was unloved, he opened her womb; but Rachel was barren. Leah conceived and bore a son, and she named him Reuben; for she said, "Because the Lord has looked on my affliction; surely now my husband will love me." She conceived again and bore a son, and said, "Because the Lord has heard that I am hated, he has given me this son also"; and she named him Simeon. Again she conceived and bore a son, and said, "Now this time my husband will be joined to me, because I have borne him three sons"; therefore he was named Levi. She conceived again and bore a son, and said, "This time I will praise the Lord"; therefore she named him Judah; then she ceased bearing. (Genesis 29:15–35)

To be attracted to two sisters in one family is one thing; for a father to trick his son-in-law into marrying the sister he is not pursuing is another. Leah was the eldest, probably almost aged out of the marrying pool, and her father was desperate to provide a husband for her. Along came Jacob, a young and virile man, handsome and self-possessed, who had had a falling out with his family and sought refuge with his uncle. The young upstart had the nerve to ask for the hand of the fairer and younger Rachel. Leah had beautiful eyes, meaning she wasn't thin and sexy enough for the likes of Jacob. But Laban, who had opened his home to this obnoxious kid, now found himself in a social and familial dilemma. The family loved having Jacob around. The girls were all over him. Laban needed the young man's labor because he couldn't manage his flocks and fields by himself anymore. He had to do something. So he concocted a plan to trick Jacob into marrying Leah. And lustful Jacob was too anxious to consummate the marriage to even take time to inspect his bride. What surprise daylight brought for him!

At the beginning of this chapter I talked about how God often used our detours and is most visible outside of the dreams we have and the plans we make. In this story we see God working around the missteps of men and women. We see their con games and their devising, and we see God pouring out compassion in the midst of their fumbling. Also in this tale we find insight into the one who would become the pillar of the faith and his struggles with love and his own identity. His struggles with his brother lead him to run away from home, and his struggles with his need for love and companionship left him indentured for a long period of his life. In the midst of all this human folly, groping and grasping, God cared for the weakest and vulnerable in this story, the women and the children, as the men bargained and plotted with their lives. We have not come so far as a society today. As I write this book, folks are occupying Wall Street and government squares and places of financial power. The powers that be plot and bargain to the detriment of the weakest and the most vulnerable still—young mothers and children—caught in the cross-fire of greed and desire.

Jacob is a progenitor of our faith and his story is intertwined with our story. He doesn't seem to be a genius when it comes to love and he seems easily manipulated by others—first his mother and then his father-in-law. He is also good at the manipulation game, but it lands him in trouble more often than not. He does seem to be good with the ladies, having spent most of his youth hanging around the tents, writing poetry, telling stories, and entertaining the women folk of his small community. He was the softer of the two brothers, and it made him more sensitive to the needs of women, which made him all that much more appealing. We watch him offer his life for love, only to be tricked and manipulated. But he hangs in there, amidst the detours and the deception, and somehow finds love and fidelity despite the overwhelming responsibility and complexities that his relationships have wrought.

Many of us find ourselves in complex situations because of our choice of partners. In our case, we were a mixed marriage both in race and in faith. In our present day it might not seem like much, but when we were married, two kids from very different faith expressions, although both Christian, were faced with some tough going and challenges from our parents and families. These many years later, we have found our way to worship together and raise our children in faith and integrity, but it required a great deal of "hanging in there," and a fidelity for love's sake that superseded culture, denomination, clan, and family.

Long after Mark and I had chosen to be a part of the Episcopal Church, and when I was early in the discernment process for priesthood, we had our daughter Ariel baptized. The priest at our parish, knowing that my father was a Presbyterian minister, invited him to vest and participate in the baptism. My father had not brought his own robe, the heavy black academic one with red piping, so the rector offered an alb to wear during the service. My dad's discomfort was palpable. He was a navy chaplain committed to inter-denominational relations and accustomed to a broad variety of worship services and styles. The clothing was another matter entirely. Yet, for love, for his daughter and granddaughter, he made the sacrifice. For love, he was willing to hang in and be drawn way outside of his comfort zone, and willing to go beyond the constraints of his traditions and culture to participate in that wonderful day.

Esther as Wonder Woman

On that day King Ahasuerus gave to Queen Esther the house of Haman, the enemy of the Jews; and Mordecai came before the king, for Esther had told what he was to her. Then the king took off his signet ring, which he had taken from Haman, and gave it to Mordecai. So Esther set Mordecai over the house of Haman.

Then Esther spoke again to the king; she fell at his feet, weeping and pleading with him to avert the evil design of Haman the Agagite and the plot that he had devised against the Jews. The king held out the golden scepter to Esther, and Esther rose and stood before the king. She said, "If it pleases the king, and if I have won his favor, and if the thing seems right before the king, and I have his approval, let an order be written to revoke the letters devised by Haman son of Hammedatha the Agagite, which he wrote giving orders to destroy the Jews who are in all the provinces of the king. For how can I bear to see the calamity that is coming on my people? Or how can I bear to see the destruction of my kindred?" Then King Ahasuerus said to Queen Esther and to the Jew Mordecai, "See, I have given Esther the house of Haman, and they have hanged him on the gallows, because he plotted to lay hands on the Jews. You may write as you please with regard to the Jews, in the name of the king, and seal it with the king's ring; for an edict written in the name of the king and sealed with the king's ring cannot be revoked." (Esther 8:1–8)

Esther isn't always listed as one of the mothers of the faith, but she should be. She goes beyond all expectations for love of her people and puts herself in harm's way for the survival of her faith and race. She gives herself for the cause. She offered her body and she offered love to the enemy so her people could survive. Hers is not an ordinary love story, but an important one, for she made a choice for love and put herself and her needs as secondary to the survival of her race and clan.

In our present day it is impossible for us to understand what was once required of young men and women when they married. Marriage was as much about economic survival as it was about attraction. We have the luxury in this day and age to marry for love, but most young people in previous generations had to marry according to station and clan. Marriages were arranged usually by men, bargaining for their families' futures. Today we are so far removed from these practices that we forget how recently laws and practices have changed. Our freedoms, especially in this country, are not those of other times and places.

We find in Esther a woman who loved God first and foremost and her people next. Because she was willing to love beyond measure, her people who should have been destroyed were saved. Her whole life was dedicated to the healing and reconciling of the nation and her people. She found her greatest strength in her faith and in her desire to heal the wounds. She put herself in harm's way so that others may thrive.

"I come from a long line of bossy women," my mother has been known to say. We Cherokees are traditionally matriarchal and matrilineal. The women were in charge of many things and the role of women in our tribe was never one of subservience to men. We saw one another as equals with different skills and responsibilities. We were all required to keep the world in balance, to walk tenderly with each other, and to guide our children carefully and respectfully. Things changed as the European population grew on this continent and our ways became subjugated and hidden. Cherokee women in leadership have always been present, and we take seriously our responsibility to be reconciled, to be in balance with all living things, as a critical part of our role. Our women have been chiefs and warriors, medicine women, artists, musicians, and healers of all sorts. One of our most important tasks the Creator has given us is to make sure that all our people are on the path of reconciliation. To reconcile, *tsunohisdodi* in Cherokee, means that we are invited to acknowledge the pain and brokenness with which we live.

Losing One's Life

I would offer myself
without a thought
without fear or misgiving
I would take the bullet
shield your body
without a worry
I would offer my life.

You offer love
without worry or fear
without counting consequence
or loss of status
without a thought
for yourself
you offer your love
for life for me.

Love hides not
doesn't hoard or clutter
love give all away
without a thought
and more love grows
life abundant
without a thought
without preparation
only offering oneself
everyday.

based on *Luke* 17:31–35

When Stalking Goes Bad

In the spring of the year, the time when kings go out to battle, David sent Joab with his officers and all Israel with him; they ravaged the Ammonites, and besieged Rabbah. But David remained at Jerusalem.

It happened, late one afternoon, when David rose from his couch and was walking about on the roof of the king's house, that he saw from the roof a woman bathing; the woman was very beautiful. David sent someone to inquire about the woman. It was reported, "This is Bathsheba daughter of Eliam, the wife of Uriah the Hittite." So David sent messengers to fetch her, and she came to him, and he lay with her. (Now she was purifying herself after her period.) Then she returned to her house. The woman conceived; and she sent and told David, "I am pregnant."

So David sent word to Joab, "Send me Uriah the Hittite." And Joab sent Uriah to David. When Uriah came to him, David asked how Joab and the people fared, and how the war was going. Then David said to Uriah, "Go down to your house, and wash your feet." Uriah went out of the king's house, and there followed him a present from the king. But Uriah slept at the entrance of the king's house with all the servants of his lord, and did not go down to his house. When they told David, "Uriah did not go down to his house," David said to Uriah, "You have just come from a journey. Why did you not go down to your house?" Uriah said to David, "The ark and Israel and Judah remain in booths; and my lord Joab and the servants of my lord are camping in the open field; shall I then go to my house, to eat and to drink, and to lie with my wife? As you live, and as your soul lives, I will not do such a thing." Then David said to Uriah, "Remain here today also, and tomorrow I will send you back." So Uriah remained in Jerusalem that day. On the next day, David invited him to eat and drink in his presence and made him drunk; and in the evening he went out to lie on his couch with the servants of his lord, but he did not go down to his house.

In the morning David wrote a letter to Joab, and sent it by the hand of Uriah. In the letter he wrote, "Set Uriah in the forefront of the hardest fighting, and then draw back from him, so that he may be struck down and die." As Joab was besieging the city, he assigned Uriah to the place where he knew there were valiant warriors. The men of the city came out and fought with Joab; and some of the servants of David among the people fell. Uriah the Hittite was killed as well. Then Joab sent and told David all the news about the fighting; and he instructed the messenger, "When you have finished telling the king all the news about the fighting, then, if the king's anger rises, and if he says to you, 'Why did you go so near the city to fight? Did you not know that they would shoot from the wall? Who killed Abimelech son of Jerubbaal? Did not a woman throw an upper millstone on him from the wall, so that he died at Thebez? Why did you go so near the wall?' then you shall say, 'Your servant Uriah the Hittite is dead too.'"

So the messenger went, and came and told David all that Joab had sent him to tell. The messenger said to David, "The men gained an advantage over us, and came out against us in the field; but we drove them back to the entrance of the gate. Then the archers shot at your servants from the wall; some of the king's servants are dead; and your servant Uriah the Hittite is dead also." David said to the messenger, "Thus you shall say to Joab, 'Do not let this matter trouble you, for the sword devours now one and now another; press your attack on the city, and overthrow it.' And encourage him."

When the wife of Uriah heard that her husband was dead, she made lamentation for him. When the mourning was over, David sent and brought her to his house, and she became his wife, and bore him a son. (2 Samuel 11)

David is always lauded for his gorgeous brilliance and leadership. His psalms are to die for. And yet, as we see in this story, David is very human. His lustful needs blind him to reality, to the laws of the land, and to feelings and needs of others. He's not using his head at all. Once the smallest boy, the poor shepherd, the runt of the litter, he is now the most powerful king in the land. He has lost all sense of boundaries and he thinks of himself as no less than God. There is danger of power, whether in ancient times or present day. We cannot read a newspaper or watch news broadcasts without hearing about a powerful person who has stepped over the line. Many think themselves above the law and take what they want—financially, sexually, and other ways—by force, believing it is their right. They lose all humility and often create their own undoing. No matter how sweet and voluptuous the fruit, it is still forbidden; they fail to "check themselves before they wreck themselves." Such was David's fatal flaw. His killing to get Bathsheeba is his undoing, the moment when he realized that the power had gone out from him, and he was no longer anything but average, much like the boy he once was. This humbling, broken place can be a new beginning. David, stripped of his false sense of pride and undone before the people and the priests, found his life and his faith again. His huge mistake became his point of redemption.

Most of us live out of the public eye but thoroughly enjoy when celebrities fall off their pedestals. The problem with our private joy at others' failings is that it makes us ever more susceptible to our own self-delusion. The more money and power we have, the more likely we are to deceive ourselves and others, thinking God will allow us to do anything we want because we are chosen, special, and anointed. How quickly the poor and wealthy alike can fall into the pit we dig with our own fantasy, our own expectations, or our lack of humility and faithfulness. We too often equate the signs of our faithfulness with wealth and power, forgetting that all that we are and have is a gift from God.

One of the real dangers faced by the leadership of any church is the temptation to allow ourselves to be put on a pedestal by parishioners. Faithful leaders are those who are not looking for devotees but rather are willing to be fully human. Many clergy people, especially gifted preachers and teachers, can mistake their stardom for the true acknowledgement from God. They equate adulation with success, and fall victim to their own advertising. God seeks humble leaders who confess their own humanity and are not persuaded of their own importance. The greatest spiritual leaders are those who are willing to be transparent, a window for others to see the heart of God.

Humbled

I thought I knew how it would work
pieces everywhere across this room scattered
across the floor broken hearts flutter
by wounded wings clasped tight
together waiting for the mending turning
a new beginning.

I thought this would be the easy part
and losing one thread we unraveled
colors everywhere tangled and frantic scrambling
to be rewoven sacred linen again.

Love mends hearts and breaks spirits aching
for healing relationship
the kiss of forgiveness the sign of peace
a touch of assurance a blessing at the end.

I thought I didn't need help, forgot
to ask include those who might know more
I lacked the soft humility of children
the wise strength of an elder and the trembling
hand outstretched of the finally honest addict.

And love will come to lift up and bind
playing a new song and putting new
wisdom in my heart, fearless love that
cast away the darkness, cuts away the envy
and replaces it with the tender laughter of
a beloved child.

based on *Luke* 18:9–14

In this chapter we have examined the stage of life we call love and adulthood. No one person has the same exact trajectory in life, especially at this stage of growth and development. We are people, human and flawed, who need to test and experiment with relationships. We play out what we have learned from our own parents—the good, bad, and the weird—and find ways to love and commit to one another. The downfall of this age is that we can live on the high of the excitement, the dating, the pursuit, the seeking, and fail to live deeply, in our own selves or with others. We have the potential to do a great deal of damage. We can permanently injure others by our selfishness and wanderlust, and we can find ourselves looking all grown up and feeling quite alone.

This can be a very difficult time in one's spiritual life as well. Many religious communities overlook the needs of the young adults, the folks in their twenties and thirties. The leadership falsely assumes that people will come back to religion when they become parents, when they need the services for baptism and marriage. At this vulnerable time in our lives, we are invited to see a time when the quest for love can invite a deepening and abiding spirituality. This age does not need to resemble a sports competition, but might instead be considered as training for life, building the emotional and spiritual muscle needed to live in a long relationship and learn to care for others.

CHAPTER 4 • REFLECTION

Exercises and Questions

1. What was (or is) it like for you when you first fall in love?

2. How do your family and friends respond to your choice in partners?

3. What struggles do you have within yourself while in relationship? (Example: self-confidence, fear of loss, time challenges)

4. What roles do culture, income, and religion have in your choice in partners?

5. How have you dealt with arguments and crisis between one another, and how does your faith come into play?

Exercises

Role play—a dating scene; going to a friend's wedding alone; party/dance disasters

Try to approach this lightly, if possible, but take turns role playing trying to share with another person, trying to ask for a dance, date, etc. Take turns in the group. Let those who are comfortable participate, and others who want to sit out can still participate as observers.

For Observers:

What do you observe about what we say to each other?

How do you feel watching this scene?

For Participants:

How did you feel saying what you did? Why did you say what you did?

What did you learn about yourself in this scenario?

For everyone:

What do we need to ask God for this week in our lives?

Aging Gracefully, Sort Of: Only Martyrs Still Look Good

However foolishly we begin our adulthood, the good news is we grow beyond our first loves and our feeble attempts to build relationships. We gain wisdom and learn to be caretakers by fits and starts and hopefully are blessed with a community that includes wise elders who help us on our way. Whether we gain strength from within or outside of our families, our middle years are signified by the ability to step outside of the basics of identity and care for others. This stage of caring, as Erikson named it, is a period when we are not so obsessed with how we look and who looks at us, but rather who is looking up to us. During this time we are creating family, nurturing children, and building businesses. We have often solidified our skills and can create new ways of being and doing. Erikson defines the challenges of this part of life as the tension between generativity and stagnation: when we struggle to balance between outward and inward care. This stage often falls between the early forties until the mid-sixties and may begin with some type of mid-life crisis. We find ourselves constantly trying to measure accomplishments and failures. We question whether we are satisfied, whether we are stuck in a rut, and wonder how we will plan for the next steps in life and care for the needs of the younger generation. We can find ourselves in times of stagnation during this period of life when we wonder whether we have made any impact or if we have done enough to help those whom we brought into the world.

In these days, gravity begins to work overtime, hair begins to turn gray, waists thicken, and we worry less about attracting a mate. We look in the mirror a little less and a little more often in the rear view at our kids or the youth we have left behind. We wonder where the time has gone as we realize we don't have the time to dwell on what is past. Our days are spent minding others: children, aging parents, our co-workers, employees, and students. We find ourselves standing by the bed, wondering what we forgot to do. Is the dog in for the night? Is it the night to take out the garbage? Did we sign the papers left on the dining table?

When I was a child, my siblings and I used to go into hysterics when we would find a dishcloth in the refrigerator and the milk bottle in the sink. We would laugh ourselves silly thinking how forgetful and goofy our mother was. Here she was, a woman with five children spanning seventeen years, who did an amazing job keeping the whole operation functioning. We found amusement in her all-out exhaustion because we had yet to stand in her shoes. We didn't see she might need our help. We just laughed until we were rolling on the floor. We teased her about it as she staggered into the kitchen to make our breakfast. Good natured and half-asleep she would smell the milk and deem it drinkable, feed us, and send us on our way in good time. We giggled all the way to school, thinking adults to be the silliest, most ridiculous creatures on the face of the earth.

Many years later, I found myself standing with the refrigerator door wide open, staring at a hairbrush on a shelf. Exhausted with my hands full, I couldn't help but laugh, and remember my mother. With our three girls, socks and hairbrushes were the most commonly lost items, and many mornings began as there was a panic as we tried to find them. My first thought was, "Ah, there it is," as if leaving a hairbrush in the refrigerator was a common experience. My second thought was about how I had misunderstood my mother. I now understand.

Little Ones

Slumbering the night air moving trees
dreams slide through the quiet startling me
awake with fear for my little ones.

Did I hear a cry in the night rising
slowing approaching heart fluttering bravery
lost to concern for these little ones.

Daylight and they wander off brave
with no brains or fear as yet darkness
settles and our nightmares begin.

I creep to the crib and all is safe breathing
lifts the sweet small chest and the breath
of an angel sour milk and freedom dreams
permeate the air.

I awake to know the heart of God beating
within mine aching to protect and shield
harboring the little ones
from those who would snatch and destroy.

Tonight the little ones are nestled warm
and snug in the heart of God and known in
a mother's trembling heart and grateful sigh.

Jesus Is Presented in the Temple, or Who's Touching my Baby?

When the time came for their purification according to the law of Moses, they brought him up to Jerusalem to present him to the Lord (as it is written in the law of the Lord, "Every firstborn male shall be designated as holy to the Lord"), and they offered a sacrifice according to what is stated in the law of the Lord, "a pair of turtle-doves or two young pigeons."

Now there was a man in Jerusalem whose name was Simeon; this man was righteous and devout, looking forward to the consolation of Israel, and the Holy Spirit rested on him. It had been revealed to him by the Holy Spirit that he would not see death before he had seen the Lord's Messiah. Guided by the Spirit, Simeon came into the temple; and when the parents brought in the child Jesus, to do for him what was customary under the law, Simeon took him in his arms and praised God, saying, "Master, now you are dismissing your servant in peace, according to your word; for my eyes have seen your salvation, which you have prepared in the presence of all peoples, a light for revelation to the Gentiles and for glory to your people Israel."

And the child's father and mother were amazed at what was being said about him. Then Simeon blessed them and said to his mother Mary, "This child is destined for the falling and the rising of many in Israel, and to be a sign that will be opposed so that the inner thoughts of many will be revealed—and a sword will pierce your own soul too."

There was also a prophet, Anna the daughter of Phanuel, of the tribe of Asher. She was of a great age, having lived with her husband for seven years after her marriage, then as a widow to the age of eighty-four. She never left the temple but worshipped there with fasting and prayer night and day. At that moment she came, and began to praise God and to speak about the child to all who were looking for the redemption of Jerusalem. (Luke 2:22–38)

Joseph and Mary took their little son to be presented in the temple. Life was pretty confusing. They were a long way from home, with no female relatives to babysit or take turns while they slept. They thought they could handle it all, but were probably completely overwhelmed. For new parents, one of the most painful and obnoxious challenges is dealing with all the older people who offer advice. Take an infant out in public and watch what people say and do. They want to touch the child, they want to tell you if your baby is so big or too small. They want to know the intimate details of the child's birth and prove what wonderful, knowledgeable parents or grandparents they are by the advice they give. Vulnerable, exhausted, and probably a little defensive, Mary and Jospeh took the boy to be blessed and they encountered Anna and Simeon. They wanted one simple day, one simple moment without interference and commentary, and here came these two ancient wonders.

Wide-eyed Simeon, delighted and swaying, took Jesus from the parents. As he quoted scripture to them, perhaps they wondered why they had chosen this day to come to the Temple. God seemed to send them into the most awkward and unusual circumstances—donkeys, stables, shepherds, and wise men—but this was the most peculiar to date. Simeon spouted beautiful words of blessing and power over the child, and then as he handed the infant back to his anxious mother who was barely more than a baby herself, he scared the dickens out of her. I can hear her now. "Joseph, did you hear what he said? A sword piercing my soul? Should I report him, I mean, was he threatening me? And you, you just stood there and let him scare me. All hairy, wild-eyed and smelly he was! Why didn't you do something?"

I imagine Joseph did a lot of shrugging, loving his wife dearly and wondering how they were going to get this boy though his childhood, especially if these first few weeks were any indication of what was to come. Their little argument on the steps of the Temple was interrupted by the oldest woman they had ever seen. Silver hair flying in all directions, a face full of age spots, and a mouth full of missing teeth, Anna assaulted them and demanded the child. The prophetess delighted in the child, singing to him and rocking him in her ancient arms. She told them she had been waiting all of her life, all of her eighty-four years, to see this child. As she released Jesus to his relieved parents she went off in a trance, singing and dancing, her skinny wrinkled arms flung high in the air.

The life stage of generativity is a time when we struggle with exhaustion, trying to get through the day, putting one foot in front of the other. We can miss the blessing because we are so worn down, so over tired that we only want to make it to the couch. We can stagnate emotionally and spiritually because there is so much to be done, so many to care for, and never enough money in the pocket or hours in the day.

I remember a Christmas when I was a fairly new parent. We had a small income and were careful about our purchases, trying to keep to a very tight budget. Our oldest daughter Emily wanted a record player of her own. I was pregnant with Ariel, our second, and more exhausted than usual as I shopped. I decided to order a record player for her from a mail order catalog. These were the days before internet, so I had to call in the order or physically go to the catalog store. I ordered a sweet little record player with a Winnie the Pooh design, perfect for her age. Late Christmas Eve as we were getting things ready for bed, we decided to check the record player box. To our horror, the record player was Disco-Pooh, complete with a set of strobe lights on the side of the contraption. I cried, knowing she would be horrified.

Christmas morning came full of wide-eyed wonder and wrapping paper. Emily loved the record player and the flashing lights, despite my horror and embarrassment. I had to admit it was exactly right, exactly what she had wanted. It was not what I had asked for or we thought she needed, but somehow it was right. We often find God when we let go of the tight control we feel we need to have and try to live in the present moment. If we judge life by our expectations, we are bound to be heartily disappointed, but God moves in the disappointment and invites us to move also from judgment to delight.

"I'm Gonna Kill You!"
or The Anxiety of the Parents

Now, day by day, Tobit kept counting how many days Tobias would need for going and for returning. And when the days had passed and his son did not appear, he said, "Is it possible that he has been detained? Or that Gabael has died, and there is no one to give him the money?" And he began to worry. His wife Anna said, "My child has perished and is no longer among the living." And she began to weep and mourn for her son, saying, "Woe is me, my child, the light of my eyes, that I let you make the journey." But Tobit kept saying to her, "Be quiet and stop worrying, my dear; he is all right. Probably something unexpected has happened there. The man who went with him is trustworthy and is one of our own kin. Do not grieve for him, my dear; he will soon be here." She answered him, "Be quiet yourself! Stop trying to deceive me! My child has perished." She would rush out every day and watch the road her son had taken, and would heed no one. When the sun had set she would go in and mourn and weep all night long, getting no sleep at all.

Now when the fourteen days of the wedding celebration had ended that Raguel had sworn to observe for his daughter, Tobias came to him and said, "Send me back, for I know that my father and mother do not believe that they will see me again. So I beg of you, father, to let me go so that I may return to my own father. I have already explained to you how I left him." But Raguel said to Tobias, "Stay, my child, stay with me; I will send messengers to your father Tobit and they will inform him about you." But he said, "No! I beg you to send me back to my father." So Raguel promptly gave Tobias his wife Sarah, as well as half of all his property: male and female slaves, oxen and sheep, donkeys and camels, clothing, money, and household goods. Then he saw them safely off;

he embraced Tobias and said, "Farewell, my child; have a safe journey. The Lord of heaven prosper you and your wife Sarah, and may I see children of yours before I die." Then he kissed his daughter Sarah and said to her, "My daughter, honor your father-in-law and your mother-in-law, since from now on they are as much your parents as those who gave you birth. Go in peace, daughter, and may I hear a good report about you as long as I live." Then he bade them farewell and let them go. Then Edna said to Tobias, "My child and dear brother, the Lord of heaven bring you back safely, and may I live long enough to see children of you and of my daughter Sarah before I die. In the sight of the Lord I entrust my daughter to you; do nothing to grieve her all the days of your life. Go in peace, my child. From now on I am your mother and Sarah is your beloved wife. May we all prosper together all the days of our lives." Then she kissed them both and saw them safely off. Tobias parted from Raguel with happiness and joy, praising the Lord of heaven and earth, King over all, because he had made his journey a success. Finally, he blessed Raguel and his wife Edna, and said, "I have been commanded by the Lord to honor you all the days of my life." (Tobit 10)

Worry and anxiety are often a part of this stage of life. We can find ourselves angry with worry, pacing when the car is out too late, and ready to pounce like a huge bear when our children finally walk through the door. Some of our fears are real and others are phantoms, stirrings that become a part of us as we find ourselves overcome by our sense of responsibility. Tobit knew how dangerous the world can be, and he feared his son Tobias wasn't aware enough. He saw his son as naïve, often experimenting and taking risks. He had been a hellcat as a boy, full of scrapes and bumps, scaring his mother to death as he hung from high branches upside down.

Tobit had lived long enough to know great loss and pain. He woke up some nights when Tobias was young and tiptoed to his cradle to make sure the child was still breathing. He didn't know if he would be able to see his son to manhood, or if this little wonder knew how frightening it was to be a parent. Fathers and sons rarely talk about the pride and fear of parenthood and the terrible, wonderful, fearful joy. Parents cannot anticipate all the challenges that will face their little ones; they do know how much they wish they could protect them. Tobit remembered those early days and he feared the worst the longer his son was gone. He fought to stay strong as Anna could not hold back the tears. Rather than give into the sorrow, all he could do was trust his son and his God.

Parents live with a great deal of anxiety for the health and welfare of their children. We deal with it in different ways, but we all have our share of worry, wondering whether we are up to the responsibility we have been given. Some parents find surrogates, read a thousand books, or educate themselves in every trendy parenting technique they can find. Others ignore the anxiety and pain, and often end up ignoring their children because they cannot face up to the anxiety and the responsibility. Parenting is a hard and exhausting task, and is often underappreciated by society. When I was first a mother in the late 1970s, people my age would shun me at parties because I had decided to stay at home with my daughter rather than being a career mother. Ten years later these same women and men came to me for advice and support.

When our daughter Ariel was in first grade, we suspected she had a problem with reading. Her teacher would reassure us and tell us how bright she was and how well she was reading. Although I saw some troubling signs, I trusted the teacher. At the end of the year they told us Ariel was not reading at grade level and would need to be kept back. I was crushed to think that our bright, wonderful little girl had tried to tell us she was struggling. Further testing showed that she was highly intelligent and severely dyslexic. The school decided she could go onto second grade because she was such a good student.

As a mother, I felt I had failed my daughter. I sobbed in the car, wondering why I had not noticed her problems, not been more careful or more attentive. I was newly ordained, trying to learn my craft, working full time, and raising three daughters. Had my selfishness, my work, my inadequacies allowed me to let her down? Fortunately, the teacher Ariel was assigned was the most amazing woman who offered another point of view. She met with us and proceeded to tell Ariel what a marvelous mind she had. "Ariel, there is nothing wrong with you" she said, "but we just haven't figured out your marvelous brain. It is my job as your teacher to find the key that opens you to learning. Will you help me find the key this year?"

Two stunned parents watched as a huge smile crept across her face. Ariel jumped up and hugged us all. One person can make all the difference. Ariel was reading at grade level by the end of that year. She learned how to deal with her challenges and graduated from college, surrounded by her beaming and joyful family.

Mother's Day

There is no peace dishes
keep piling voices raising needs
unending silence only
in the dead of night.

There is no finish day flows
into night homework and games spill
everywhere underfoot tripping
arm loads of wash done piling
up again.

There is no peace sweeter
newborn breath asleep arms limp
trusting completely a heartbeat
familiar and constant pounding
with love bursting
with joy.

There is no terror bigger
than the first permit toddler
grown sitting behind the wheel

heart breaking with fear
hands trembling in prayer.

There is no greater gift
the precious life observed
shared, complicated and challenged,
a child for a mother
peace and joy amidst mess
high volume love unceasing
God presence known, incarnate
love made real.

Peter and Cornelius, or Just Eat it!

In Caesarea there was a man named Cornelius, a centurion of
the Italian Cohort, as it was called. He was a devout man who
feared God with all his household; he gave alms generously
to the people and prayed constantly to God. One afternoon
at about three o'clock he had a vision in which he clearly saw
an angel of God coming in and saying to him, "Cornelius."
He stared at him in terror and said, "What is it, Lord?" He
answered, "Your prayers and your alms have ascended as a
memorial before God. Now send men to Joppa for a certain
Simon who is called Peter; he is lodging with Simon, a tanner,
whose house is by the seaside." When the angel who spoke
to him had left, he called two of his slaves and a devout sol-
dier from the ranks of those who served him, and after telling
them everything, he sent them to Joppa.

About noon the next day, as they were on their journey and
approaching the city, Peter went up on the roof to pray. He
became hungry and wanted something to eat; and while it
was being prepared, he fell into a trance. He saw the heaven
opened and something like a large sheet coming down, being
lowered to the ground by its four corners. In it were all kinds
of four-footed creatures and reptiles and birds of the air. Then

he heard a voice saying, "Get up, Peter; kill and eat." But Peter said, "By no means, Lord; for I have never eaten anything that is profane or unclean." The voice said to him again, a second time, "What God has made clean, you must not call profane." This happened three times, and the thing was suddenly taken up to heaven.

Now while Peter was greatly puzzled about what to make of the vision that he had seen, suddenly the men sent by Cornelius appeared. They were asking for Simon's house and were standing by the gate. They called out to ask whether Simon, who was called Peter, was staying there. While Peter was still thinking about the vision, the Spirit said to him, "Look, three men are searching for you. Now get up, go down, and go with them without hesitation; for I have sent them." So Peter went down to the men and said, "I am the one you are looking for; what is the reason for your coming?" They answered, "Cornelius, a centurion, an upright and God-fearing man, who is well spoken of by the whole Jewish nation, was directed by a holy angel to send for you to come to his house and to hear what you have to say." So Peter invited them in and gave them lodging.

The next day he got up and went with them, and some of the believers from Joppa accompanied him. The following day they came to Caesarea. Cornelius was expecting them and had called together his relatives and close friends. On Peter's arrival Cornelius met him, and falling at his feet, worshipped him. But Peter made him get up, saying, "Stand up; I am only a mortal." And as he talked with him, he went in and found that many had assembled; and he said to them, "You yourselves know that it is unlawful for a Jew to associate with or to visit a Gentile; but God has shown me that I should not call anyone profane or unclean. So when I was sent for, I came without objection. Now may I ask why you sent for me?"

Cornelius replied, "Four days ago at this very hour, at three o'clock, I was praying in my house when suddenly a man in dazzling clothes stood before me. He said, 'Cornelius, your prayer has been heard and your alms have been remembered before God. Send therefore to Joppa and ask for Simon, who is called Peter; he is staying in the home of Simon, a tanner, by the sea.' Therefore I sent for you immediately, and you have been kind enough to come. So now all of us are here in the presence of God to listen to all that the Lord has commanded you to say." (Acts 10)

Not everything we do in this time of our lives involves children, as many of us are not involved in parenting but are still building for the next generation. I include the story of Peter and Cornelius, because it speaks about mentoring and being a mentor, two important roles at this stage. When we are at our best, we share our skills and wisdom with the next generation, setting the stage for their success and innovation. At our worst, we are bound by our upbringing, fearful of innovation and difference, and we spend our energy trying to make the younger folks conform rather than teaching them to strengthen skills and deepen wisdom. There is great danger when we try to make the next generation into our own image, a mirror reflection devoid of their divinely inspired uniqueness.

Peter was a mess of a man. He had love and compassion for anyone God sent his way. He was a good Jew, a skilled and successful fisherman, and a loving father, husband, and son. He was also a famous disciple, the one to whom Jesus had said, "on this rock I will build my church." Peter was the man Jesus called Satan, the one who denied the Savior when the going got tough, and the disciple most likely to blurt out something incredibly impulsive. Peter was a human, made of flesh and blood, conflicted and often confused, a product of his culture, gender, and age.

Peter had stopped at a hostel for a rest on his journey when he fell into a trance waiting for dinner. All sorts of forbidden food were put before him and he was horrified. He was on his way to meet Cornelius and he already was leery. The man was faithful but foreign and Peter didn't take well to foreigners and their strange ways, especially their food and music. He had kept the Jewish dietary laws all his life. Now God was putting sin and temptation in his way, right in front of a starving fisherman. Peter was troubled. He had to ponder for quite a while to grasp what God would have him do. When the time came, he sat down to dinner and ate what Cornelius served.

God would have us learn lessons from complicated situations, to continue to grow, and welcome innovation and difference as divine gifts. Peter struggled to embrace innovation and differences and learn from the foreigner. Cornelius offered the invitation, after listening to God in his dream. Peter learned from one he had not expected God to use: "God has shown me that I should not call anyone profane or unclean." The Gentile he once considered untouchable became his teacher. If we are truly caring for the younger generation, God can use the relationship to grow the mentor and the student together. If we are willing to be uncomfortable with the new and innovative, we might just find God in our midst, teaching and renewing us in ways we could not even imagine.

When I was made bishop, our daughter Phoebe was in seventh grade. We enrolled her at mid-year in an Episcopal girls' school in Richmond, knowing it would be a tough transition for her. Middle school is difficult enough without having to move in the middle of a term. Having a mother who was a bishop added to the awkwardness and embarrassment. She was brave her first few days, and the teachers and administration did their all to help her. After several weeks she got in the car raging mad. She was tired of being called a Yankee or being teased about being Native. She was offended by the assumptions others made about her. They were defining her based on stereotypes and ignorance. Her hurt was palpable. We talked for a long time about how to respond. I offered to go to the head of the school and challenge the girls' behavior. Phoebe made it clear that would embarrass her, and decided to deal with it in her own way.

Throughout her junior high and high school years we talked about how to handle prejudice and false assumptions. During her junior and senior years she had the opportunity to do a winter-term internship in New York, working alongside the Anglican Observer at the UN, Deacon Tai, who was Samoan. She met with women concerned with the plight of girls in third world countries. She suggested they include girls to their meetings if they wanted to understand their needs. The practice continues to this day. Phoebe graduated, leading her class side by side with her best friend who was African American. She had found ways in her five years to make ignorance and assumption into an educational process for herself and her class. In the best of times, when we are opening our hearts and truly yearning to be open, the teacher can learn from the student, and the whole community is lifted up because of the growth. Our uniqueness and our individuality can be blessings to the whole.

God truly is "no respecter of persons" as the King James Bible reads, but we are often judging and too often dismissing folks who are different. My husband's only uncle was a wonderful, faithful man who had wanted to be a priest. He, however, had a deformed hand. Brilliant and humble, he sought a role in the church, but was sent away because he was not perfect. In the Catholic Church of the 1940s, a priest had to be physically perfect in order to represent Jesus properly. "Unc," as he was affectionately called, went on to be a very successful chemist, a wonderful man, and a true leader of people. He was loved by many and cared for his family and friends with great kindness. Throughout his life he remained a devout Catholic, never letting his rejection from Holy Orders keep him from loving and serving God. The church lost a great servant because they could not see past their own blindness and prejudice. As we remember God is no respecter of persons, we are invited to think again about who and what we think are acceptable to God. The Creator invites us to be creative and inclusive with ourselves and with our world.

Not Like You

I am not the usual sort nor
are you and we had our hosts
of troubles and turn downs
had to make our living any old way.

Not the prize pupil nor the model
child of want and neglect fierce
with love and loyalty among the riffraff
we are trusted like saints.

The Pharisees look down their patrician noses
in daylight revered feared in the dark
making and breaking pawns, toying with confident
youth who become slaves to the fashion
and lose to their darkness.

We walk in broken down shoes
spent laces and tattered jeans
along dusty highways we hear singing
and we run to the well with joy.

We will not be afraid although darkness comes
too often to human leaders' hearts
to people who mouth spirit and inhabit
the mildew of their own violent needs.

We will run in rain and sorrow
in tall grass and deep mud
the spirit calls our hearts and tugs us
beyond circumstances and maps
beyond race or class
to a sanctuary made of love
and fired with compassion and welcome.

based on John 4:7–26

In this chapter we have explored how people care for the younger generation and how they share their wisdom and skills with others. Though these might seem like practical tasks with no real spiritual nature, I am persuaded that nurturing others and raising up our next generation are critical tasks. We were formed in faith by those who came before us; who we are has been shaped by the environments we grew up in. When we grow up surrounded by caring and encouragement, there are few limits to how we can grow and thrive. If we are thwarted and crushed as we try to grow, we can struggle with the burdens of hopelessness and fear.

My ancestors knew that the whole community was responsible for the spiritual development of their youth, and all the adults took seriously their roles and responsibilities. The Cherokee Stomp Dance demonstrates this commitment to raising up and teaching the whole community together. It begins at dawn when a Firekeeper and his assistant begin to build a fire that needs to last through the dance. The Firekeeper starts with a "sponge" (small slivers of wood from the innermost part of an oak tree) and uses a rock and flint to make a spark. All fire is sacred to traditional Cherokees, but this one has unique importance. It is our custom to dig a pit and build the fire at the bottom, tending it constantly. As the sun rises, the men sit around the fire talking about political issues and the women prepare a meal for the day consisting of both traditional and modern food.

The fire is surrounded by seven arbors and each arbor represents one of these seven clans: Wolf; Wild Potato; Paint; Bird; Long Hair or Twister or Wind; and Blind Savannah or Blue. Later in the afternoon, sermons are given in the Cherokee language that focus on having love for all people and creation. After the sermons, they play stickball, which is an ancient Cherokee game similar to lacrosse. The preaching often goes on until the sunset. The ceremonial pipe is passed to each clan member who takes seven puffs before passing it on. The chief, medicine men, and elders gather for a meeting, eventually calling for the first dance of the night, which is by invitation only and features the tribal elders, medicine men, and the heads of clans. The second call to dance includes a leader, the assistants, and one or more "shell-shakers" who wear leg rattles traditionally made out of turtle shells filled with pebbles. Today some use cans filled with pebbles to provide rhythmic accompaniment as they dance around the fire. The ceremonial observance involves sacrifices made by the ceremonial leaders, prayers, taking medicine, going to water or river for ritual cleansing, and smoking of the pipe. Participants visit, feast, and dance far into the night. The Stomp Dance is considered to be a holy event for worshiping *U-ne-tla-nv* (God, The Creator). There is no littering, no consumption of liquor, and no rowdy behavior of any kind. The rules are written in the Cherokee language and posted on a board hung up for the public to see.

These traditions are our ways of teaching our young to learn from one another. Sometimes misunderstood as simply a social gathering, the Stomp Dance is treated with great reverence and is essential for understanding the history, present and future, of our people. The holy is in the midst of us when we are doing both the simple, daily tasks of sharing with and tending the younger generations. The holy is also present when we gather in church and when we reach out in love to the stranger in our communities.

CHAPTER 5 • REFLECTION

Exercises and Questions

1. What was your experience of learning as a child?

2. Who did you consider your best teacher? Why?

3. How did your culture and family shape you?

4. Describe a time when someone broke down your assumptions and changed you attitude towards another person or group of people.

5. What conditions help you be most open and which invite you to shut down?

Group Exercise

The set-up for this meeting might include having large sheets of drawing paper, markers, paints, and other art media for people to experiment with. Time can be set aside to draw, write, or paint. Asking how do we open ourselves to others and how do we protect the most vulnerable among us, folks can have time to express themselves in any way they chose. The artwork can be displayed in the room, and everyone who wishes can take a turn explaining what they were expressing.

Prayer—facing the artwork, each person can offer a short petition for themselves and for all those who are teaching, learning, being mentors, etc. They can also name their mentors and teachers in this prayer.

Embracing the Child of God: Time to Run with Scissors

In this final chapter we will look at the gifts of age and see that we have come full circle to embrace the love and delights of our inner child. We will examine a few encouraging stories about God's desire for us to embrace our unique gifts and to live a life of faith formed by an authentic understanding of our mortality and God's infinite love. Erikson describes these later years—from the mid-sixties to death—as the age of wisdom: a time when we find the capacity to integrate our ego and check it at the door (as it were) as we deal with the very daily challenges of growing older. We can choose to embrace our mortality and give away our wisdom and joy, or we can become bitter, unhappy, and dissatisfied with what we have accomplished or failed to accomplish. We can reflect on the past and conclude we are finally satisfied with our lives, or we can choose to be angry over what we have not been or done.

Several years ago, while I was serving a parish in Delaware, I had a misunderstanding with my mother over one of my children. She had treated my child inappropriately, I thought, and I was consumed with anger. I didn't speak to my her for several months. One day, a woman came to visit me for pastoral counseling. She told me a tale about herself and her daughter. The woman was close to my mother's age and spun a story of a gradual breakdown in relationship that had spiraled down through decades. She could not remember the original issue and she was afraid she would never see her daughter again. Her heart was broken. I encouraged her to seek out her daughter, and told her it was never too late for God to mend their broken hearts. Then it hit me: I was talking to myself. I could choose to make it right, to grow up and act like a mature adult. I was the one burdened with anger, the one aching to be loved and forgiven. That woman did reconcile with her daughter. I went home and called my mother, and the pain and anger that I was holding melted away. The woman who came to my office was a messenger from God to me, even though I thought I was the one who was being helped, God gave me the gift of new insight and a new heart.

In this final stage of our lives, we have the opportunity to be completely transparent and open. The games and false pretenses of our earlier lives are useless. The wrinkles and the years have overtaken our false pride. Elders are shameless, willing to tell it like it is. We will examine a few powerful stories from the Bible and invite God to speak to us about the fullness of life and the gifts of age.

When?

> I had a dream last night woke
> hoping that I was invited to dance dust
> rising on the pow wow grounds shrill song
> spinning for lips young and old
> ancient with the old hurts born anew
> with hopes flying for my young.
>
> I had a dream that courage pulsed fearless
> joy for a new beginning for an old dance songs
> on lips morning light revealing creation
> opening a day with an imprint of God on my heart.
>
> I had a dream that a complete people free
> of crutches and addictions baggage off loaded

symptoms eradicated by radical love streams
of clear water renewing fleshing out hidden
skin, tender places no longer.

I had a dream and heard you dreaming and God
dreamed a people free songs rising on our lips
morning no longer mourning light no longer shadow
day full of spirit renewed, reconciled dancing
on our sacred ground where God is found.

Breaking a Hip: All in a Day's Work

The hand of the Lord came upon me, and he brought me out by the spirit of the Lord and set me down in the middle of a valley; it was full of bones. He led me all round them; there were very many lying in the valley, and they were very dry. He said to me, "Mortal, can these bones live?" I answered, "O Lord God, you know." Then he said to me, "Prophesy to these bones, and say to them: O dry bones, hear the word of the Lord. Thus says the Lord God to these bones: I will cause breath to enter you, and you shall live. I will lay sinews on you, and will cause flesh to come upon you, and cover you with skin, and put breath in you, and you shall live; and you shall know that I am the Lord."

So I prophesied as I had been commanded; and as I prophesied, suddenly there was a noise, a rattling, and the bones came together, bone to its bone. I looked, and there were sinews on them, and flesh had come upon them, and skin had covered them; but there was no breath in them. Then he said to me, "Prophesy to the breath, prophesy, mortal, and say to the breath: Thus says the Lord God: Come from the four winds, O breath, and breathe upon these slain, that they may live." I prophesied as he commanded me, and the breath came into them, and they lived, and stood on their feet, a vast multitude.

Then he said to me, "Mortal, these bones are the whole house of Israel. They say, "Our bones are dried up, and our hope is lost; we are cut off completely." Therefore prophesy, and say to them, Thus says the Lord God: I am going to open your graves, and bring you up from your graves, O my people; and I will bring you back to the land of Israel. And you shall know that I am the Lord, when I open your graves, and bring you up from your graves, O my people. I will put my spirit within you, and you shall live, and I will place you on your own soil; then you shall know that I, the Lord, have spoken and will act, says the Lord." (Ezekiel 37)

The story of the valley of dry bones gave me the creeps as a kid, yet I really kind of liked it for some strange reason. A picture of despair, and life long ago ended: old bleached-out dry bones, the detritus from some folks who were long dead were lying out in the sun, wedged between weeds and rocks. In my imagination, the picture has always been in black and white, a bad dream that only gets worse. We are all mortals, but many of us do not like to talk about death; we often pretend that we will live a long life, seemingly forever. Even faithful people shun going to visit the sick in the hospital, attending a funeral, or even visiting a grave-yard as though these acts will somehow hasten their end. Many people have an aversion to lingering among these reminders and symbols of their mortality.

The same fears may be at the heart of the avoidance behavior often directed at the elderly in our country. Our old folks remind us of our frailty, vulnerability, and mortality so we put them away in institutions where they are with people like them and out of our sight. We don't go to them for advice or inspiration or consider them sources of new life. We fear what we will become so we do our best to ignore the people who gave their lives for us, who toiled and fought, who were once young and virile and never thought of themselves as old.

Several years ago, our daughter Phoebe spent the summer with my mother, working to save money for college and enjoying friends and the beach. I went to spend a few days with them for no special reason. My mother's arm began swelling up and she was rightly concerned. A neighbor and friend who was a doctor took a look at her and suggested she get it checked out. It was a Friday evening in July and, although I was ready to hunker down and read, I agreed to drive her to the Emergency Room, which was about fifteen miles away. I took my book knowing that it could be a long wait on a summer weekend night. As we were traveling up the parkway, fireworks were going off in a nearby town. We were remarking about the fireworks when we struck two deer—or rather they struck us as they fled the noise in the distance. The airbags deployed and I somehow managed to guide the car over to the shoulder. I was okay but concerned about my eighty-five-year-old mom. She was healthy but I was anxious and afraid that she might had been hurt. She was okay she said, just shook up.

I called 911 and explained that we had hit two deer and that the car looked totaled. I also told them we were already en route to the hospital when it had happened. I prayed they would respond quickly and they did. Two competent EMTs got us in the ambulance after I had spoken with the two officers who also arrived. We were shaky but relieved that everyone had been so prompt and efficient. As they wheeled my mother into the ER, someone shouted, "Is this the eighty-five-year-old woman?"

"Yes, we have the eighty-five-year-old woman with us and all vital signs are good!" My mother turned to me from the wheelchair and gave me a look that could melt paint. She was furious and embarrassed. If looks could kill, I would have fainted dead away that night. The ER was jammed and it took a while for us get into an exam room. When we finally got a room, she said, "Did you have to tell them I was eighty-five?" I shrugged, trying to come up with a valid answer to explain why I had told the truth. When I had no answer, I pleaded to be excused to go call the family. She had cooled down some when I returned and I learned you cannot always do a favor for a family member. Though we laugh about the incident now, she still maintains I was out of line.

Aging demands a different kind of strength than that of our youth. We have to come to terms with an enormous amount of loss, as well as physical and mental changes that can be frustrating, and even debilitating. All of us need dignity and community to thrive, yet we are often robbed of both as we age. Our friends leave us, our children grow lives of their own, and we feel less and less useful. We spend a great deal of time with doctors and nurses who evaluate our physical condition. We often lack the physical contact we took for granted in our middle years. The children who used to climb up in our laps are now the stern daughters and sons who try to be helpful but end up hurting our feelings. The world seems to have left us behind, ignoring our wisdom and insight, our long view, and our ability to still dream.

The ICU and Other Fun Places: The Valley of Dry Bones Continued

The word of the Lord came to me: Mortal, take a stick and write on it, "For Judah, and the Israelites associated with it"; then take another stick and write on it, "For Joseph (the stick of Ephraim) and all the house of Israel associated with it"; and join them together into one stick, so that they may become one in your hand. And when your people say to you, "Will you not show us what you mean by these?" say to them, Thus says the Lord God: I am about to take the stick of Joseph (which is in the hand of Ephraim) and the tribes of Israel associated with it; and I will put the stick of Judah upon it, and make them one stick, in order that they may be one in my hand. When the sticks on which you write are in your hand before their eyes, then say to them, Thus says the Lord God: I will take the people of Israel from the nations among which they have gone, and will gather them from every quarter, and bring them to their own land. I will make them one nation in the land, on the mountains of Israel; and one king shall be king over them all. Never again shall they be two nations, and never again shall they be divided into two kingdoms. They shall never again defile themselves with their idols and their detestable things, or with any of their transgressions. I will save them from all the apostasies into which they have fallen, and will cleanse them. Then they shall be my people, and I will be their God.

My servant David shall be king over them; and they shall all have one shepherd. They shall follow my ordinances and be careful to observe my statutes. They shall live in the land that I gave to my servant Jacob, in which your ancestors lived; they and their children and their children's children shall live there forever; and my servant David shall be their prince forever. I will make a covenant of peace with them; it shall be an ever-lasting covenant with them; and I will bless them and multiply them, and will set my sanctuary among them for evermore. My dwelling-place shall be with them; and I will be their God, and they shall be my people. Then the nations shall know that I the Lord sanctify Israel, when my sanctuary is among them for evermore. (Ezekiel 37:15–38)

This incredible piece of narrative describes the place where our real fear and the power of God meet at the intersection of our humanity and God's divinity. We will all be dry bones some day—that is certain—but even as we decay, God is acting on our behalf, restoring, renewing, and invigorating us and all who follow after us. God breathed life into the ancients and invites us to receive the breath of new life also. Our Creator does not give up on us no matter what we face today: misery, pain, or loss. God is moving over the dark and deep to heal and renew all of humanity. Ezekiel reminds us that there is no one outside of the care and reach of our loving Creator. God's vision and scope are far beyond anything we can imagine, spanning time and space and even the limitations of our imagination and creativity.

A couple of days after the accident, I got a panicked call from my daughter Phoebe. A neighbor told her my mother had been taken to the hospital by ambulance. They also told her that her grandmother had fallen and had lost a great deal of blood. When the call came I was standing in line at the Motor Vehicles Department. I was shaken to the core by the news and took it out on the people at the DMV. I realized how petty and ridiculous I had been, getting short in the process of getting license plates. They finally handed me the plates and I went as fast as I could on the Garden State Parkway.

When I got to the emergency room that afternoon, my mother was on a stretcher near the end of the row in a fully packed ER. Her face was covered in blood, and she looked disoriented and frail. I fought back tears as I gently embraced her so as not to disturb her protective collar. She had been through x-rays and was waiting for a doctor. It really felt like this was the end. I asked her what I could do for her. She said she wanted to get cleaned up a bit. I found a washcloth and warm water and washed her face, arms, and other places where blood was visible. I couldn't help but think of all the times she must have done the same for me. To return the gift of such a simple task felt holy.

A nurse interrupted to wheel my mother off for yet another test. My mother panicked, grabbed the sheet, and pulled it up over her nose. She startled me with her movements so I tagged along, worried she was too disoriented and confused. As we waited I asked her why she pulled the sheet up. She was holding it tight over her mouth as she answered. "I know a lot of people around here. I don't want anyone to see me without my teeth in!" I knew right then she was going to pull through and provide me with new challenges and lessons for years to come.

When we live a long life, we are challenged by the limitations of a declining body, the diminishment of our faculties, and the accumulation of losses. The world swirls around us and then passes us by. The importance of retaining our dignity and our inclusion is crucial, not only for those of us who age but for society as a whole. Our elders have so much to offer us. We miss many blessings by setting them aside.

In traditional Native societies our elders are revered, and very little is accomplished unless our elders give their approval. The Cherokee National Archives reveal that J.P. Evans wrote in 1835 about the women's dance, and his insight helps us to understand the critical role that elders played in all parts of traditional Cherokee society.

> When the hour of dancing arrives, an old man, generally the eldest in a clan or town, commences singing a dirge-like air, and beating on a skin stretched over the end of a keg. Like all Cherokee air, it does not possess much variety; some parts, however, are a little touching, and add somewhat to the gloomy feelings produced by surrounding objects, on the mind of one accustomed to civilized society. Before the old man has spent much time tuning his pipes, two or three women came forward, with terrapin shells on their legs, and keep time by stamping, moving around the fire with peculiar facility, and apparent ease; in a short time most of the women present, join in the dance. This ceremony is continued as long as the whim of the old man prompts him to sing. After resting a half hour, the singing is commenced again, by the same or another old man, and the dancers again enter the circle. The night is generally wound up with a common dance.

As we find ways in our present age to include elders in our daily lives, to listen to their wisdom and be touched by them, we invite creative and renewing possibilities in our communities. Our elders and the saints who have gone before us have created a well-worn path rutted by thousands of feet and tears. We are not alone, even when we think we are. We are surrounded with "so great a cloud of witnesses" that fought for us, prayed for us, and lead us to the time and place where God will invite us to walk alongside all the previous generations.

Walking On Water—A Song for Our Times

We are so often afraid
the night winds stir up
the terrors of the day life
embittered with loss and pain
tangled in the dark dreams
the failure missteps and bitter
words screamed in hurt and anger.

He comes walking on the water
hand outstretched reaching
for you and me calming
the winds and the waves
tenderly holding us as we weep.

We are so often shadowed
our indiscretions our shame
we hide away the broken shards
the debris of our failures
from the light of day.

He comes walking on the water
hand outstretched reaching
for you and me calming
the winds and the waves
tenderly holding us as we pray.

We often kneel in the darkness
sinking deep in despair nothing
left to anchor our dreams
nothing left to cover our need
nothing left to shelter our hearts.

He comes walking on the water
hand outstretched reaching
for you and me calming
the winds and the waves
tenderly holding us as we beg.

Often with the sunrise we find
a glimpse of hope a ray

of possibility a song
on the wind accompanying the leaves
dancing in the wind.

He comes walking on the water
hand outstretched reaching
for you and me calming
the winds and the waves
tenderly holding us as we crawl.

And often we finally let go
and trust with tender steps
hopeful and tenuous and lurching
we find a rhythm forgiveness
and undeserved abundance
with each new day.

He comes walking on the water
hand outstretched reaching
for you and me calming
the winds and the waves
tenderly holding us as we dance.

Knocking on Heaven's Door: Letting Love Take Over

Let mutual love continue. Do not neglect to show hospitality to strangers, for by doing that some have entertained angels without knowing it. Remember those who are in prison, as though you were in prison with them; those who are being tortured, as though you yourselves were being tortured. Let marriage be held in honor by all, and let the marriage bed be kept undefiled; for God will judge fornicators and adulterers. Keep your lives free from the love of money, and be content with what you have; for he has said, "I will never leave you or forsake you." So we can say with confidence, "The Lord is my helper; I will not be afraid. What can anyone do to me?"

Remember your leaders, those who spoke the word of God to you; consider the outcome of their way of life, and imitate their faith. Jesus Christ is the same yesterday and today and for ever. Do not be carried away by all kinds of strange teachings; for it is well for the heart to be strengthened by grace, not by regulations about food, which have not benefited those who observe them. We have an altar from which those who officiate in the tent have no right to eat. For the bodies of those animals whose blood is brought into the sanctuary by the high priest as a sacrifice for sin are burned outside the camp. Therefore Jesus also suffered outside the city gate in order to sanctify the people by his own blood. Let us then go to him outside the camp and bear the abuse he endured. For here we have no lasting city, but we are looking for the city that is to come. Through him, then, let us continually offer a sacrifice of praise to God, that is, the fruit of lips that confess his name. Do not neglect to do good and to share what you have, for such sacrifices are pleasing to God.

Obey your leaders and submit to them, for they are keeping watch over your souls and will give an account. Let them do this with joy and not with sighing—for that would be harmful to you. Pray for us; we are sure that we have a clear conscience, desiring to act honorably in all things. I urge you all the more to do this, so that I may be restored to you very soon. Now may the God of peace, who brought back from the dead our Lord Jesus, the great shepherd of the sheep, by the blood of the eternal covenant, make you complete in everything good so that you may do his will, working among us that which is pleasing in his sight, through Jesus Christ, to whom be the glory for ever and ever. Amen.

I appeal to you, brothers and sisters, bear with my word of exhortation, for I have written to you briefly. I want you to know that our brother Timothy has been set free; and if he comes in time, he will be with me when I see you. Greet all your leaders and all the saints. Those from Italy send you greetings. Grace be with all of you. (Hebrews 13)

Paul's words came towards the end of his ministry. He had not always been so loving and caring, being the original religious storm trooper. Before he was first converted, Paul rounded up followers of Christ and sentenced them to death. He thought of himself as righteous and was determined to bring religion back into the correct and proper alignment. The Christians were messing everything up, persuading people to follow the Christ. Paul was going to stop them. When he came to Christ, he brought that same vigorous intensity to his ministry. There are many stories about the divisions and arguments he had with the disciples and other church leaders. To say he was bull-headed would be an understatement.

We all grow and learn, and Paul was no exception. The lessons from his missionary journeys, prison, and the consequences of broken relationships brought him to a different understanding of his ministry. As he aged, he saw his frailty as a gift and his own vulnerability as more room for God to work through him. He stopped trying to be absolutely right and let God remake him in the image of love. In this passage Paul was tender and loving, asking the recipients of his letter to care for each other with constant forgiveness, reconciliation, and love. He mellowed as he aged and perhaps was able to see how his aggressive nature might have done more damage than good. He invited a new kind of posture, by assuming that posture for himself. He came to a place of humility and invited all sorts of people to participate in the life of faith together.

My Cherokee ancestors also considered reconciliation to be a faithful response to God's love and presence in their lives. *Tsunohisdodi* in Cherokee—reconciliation—is an invitation to a place where we acknowledge the pain and brokenness with which we have lived. The Cherokee talk of having an ordeal disease, a spell often placed on by a parent or mentor, to strengthen an individual. Four ravens, red, black, white, and blue, are called upon to put the ordeal away—to tuck it into a crevice, *Sanigilagi*—and hide it far away forever. The Sanigilagi is the Cherokee actual name for Whiteside Mountain in North Carolina and also stands for any high and faraway place. We are people who are used to ordeals and know we are sometimes strengthened by them. The Trail of Tears, the forced removal of the Cherokee People from our ancestral home-lands in the late 1830s, was the first of many ordeals that brought us to our knees and turned us on one another. We were broken for a time but have called on our faith, our traditions, and our leaders. We found faithful ways together to be renewed and come out stronger than before. But we also know that there are events and circum-stances that must be reconciled, which is a harder path that requires relationships of openness and trust. I have learned from my elders that we are not truly weakened by ordeal and hardship but by the brokenness of relationships and structures. To reconcile is to take time to remake ourselves and our structures so there is room for all, and honor and respect for all. It is a holy discipline we are invited to engage in at all stages of our lives.

Many of us find ourselves in situations that are not reconciled within our families, our faith communities, and in our work places. Wherever two human beings are in close proximity, they will find ways to both connect and conflict. These tensions can either become fuel for destruction or the seeds of rebirth and imagination. The sparks of conflict can also provide sparks of larger human capacity and expression. We can dream ourselves into new and more complex narratives, stories which incorporate more possibilities than walls. We can learn from our elders that being reconciled is a holy activity, and any effort we put into reconciliation will be rewarded in ways we can never imagine.

The Wisdom of Peacemaking

Now is the time when the four winds subside
with the early morning stillness lingering
sleep still heavy in the eyes, gentle words
and language flow, we are like children
stretching for the day.

The storms drove us away and apart
we groaned with labor and striving
we thought we could judge and exclude
we thought we knew we were right
and in losing meekness and humility
we lost our way.

The ancestors cried out and the winds blew
we didn't listen then we tightened our grasp
we bullied and argued we flexed and raged
the dangers of an angry heart clouding all.

And the sea rose high the waves covered us
sweeping us to the four corners of the earth
and in our isolation we knew our need
in our lonely ache we knew desire for love
in our damp abandoned selves we found God.

And whispering in the wind
God loves us
in the sweet smell of new grass
God judges us with forgiveness
with the eyes of a tender parent
ready to forgive, arms ready for embrace
love aching to be made whole.

As we conclude this chapter, I invite you to imagine a new tapestry for your life. The riches and challenges of our families provide us with many ways to have deeper conversations with the scriptures and with God in prayer. We can find affinity with the ancients, who struggled and strived as we do, within families, within cultures and communities and found ways to move forward with God's help. The elders that went before us have known so many struggles and challenges, and they too have created inventive ways to live a life of faith in their own time. We can tap their deep wisdom and seed a new vision of faith within our own lives and in our families.

CHAPTER 6 • REFLECTION

Exercises and Questions

1. What do you want to like when you are very old?

2. Who taught you about life?

3. Describe an elder who shared their wisdom with you.

4. How will you tell your story when you are an elder?

5. How has God worked in your life to this point?

6. What story from scripture resonates today with your life?

Exercises:

1. This exercise can be done in one session or become more elaborate, as you choose. Find a scripture passage that really has helped you in recent times, and find a way to this story, with your story woven into it. For a single session, this might be sharing of stories. If the group would like, folks might make videos, music, dance, or art pieces to share.

2. Interview an elder. An individual or a group might want to contact older church members, grandparents,

or folks in a nursing home to interview. Simply ask them to talk about their lives, their faith, and their family of origin. It can be recorded, with permission, to share with the group or even an adult forum or class.

✑ Conclusion ✑

At the beginning of this book, I invited us to imagine, understand, and articulate our faith through that filter of our families and to understand that God is active within our frailties and complexities. No one family or community is exactly alike, but we can deepen our relationship with God as we understand ourselves in relation to others. These relationships show us the love of God, no matter how convoluted the demonstration might be. We can extract the precious gold of creation from the messiest family tables and invite God to take our small offerings and transform them into incredible works of art.

This book is intended as a starting place: a simple invitation to make holy what has been profane for so many. I have written this book to invite you to see God working in the midst of the housework and homework, rather than somewhere outside the fray; to imagine God richly in the complexity of your environment, in the context of your family, however odd or normal that family might seem. God is not found in the crystal perfection of outer space or some Hollywood version of heaven, but rather right where we are, in the here and now, in these broken bodies, these aging vessels, and in the dark places we all fear to go.

My prayer is that this book has encouraged you to be lovingly reckless, engaging in theology in all sorts of unusual places—especially right in the midst of dishes and diaper duty. My prayer is that you feel empowered to wrestle with the Scriptures, using all the imagination at your disposal. God wants to be understood and known in your context, and is willing to dance in your imagination and find a common language so that you might invite the Creator within.